"Each page contains life-giving truths tha
to lead an organization that's been ravag(
lacked emotional agility. I am confident in my abilities as an
emotionally agile leader, and I am excited to implement the
practical applications from this book in our organization.

I'm thankful to Kevin for being faithful to write on the days
he didn't feel like writing so that I, along with others, would
have this survival guide to navigate challenging times on our
journey as emotionally agile leaders."

—Brian Schaffer, CEO,
Crossroads Ministry of Estes Park

"For young people, this book contains a wealth of information
that they should read, digest, and practice. Rather than simply
learning by their mistakes, young readers can draw from this
book to navigate the dangerous minefield of developing into
successful leaders of people and organizations. If read properly,
The Emotionally Agile Leader becomes a how-to book to accelerate
one's leadership development.

Kevin's perspective would have helped me a great deal
as a young man—it is exactly the type of read that I should
have undertaken. As an old man, this book reminds me to be
intentional as I interact with my colleagues (professionally and
personally). Old dogs sometimes fall into bad habits, and this
book is a strong reminder that one should never stop working
at becoming a great leader."

—Glenn Bryan, MBA, DBA,
Ohio Wesleyan University

"A must-read . . . Kevin has beautifully revealed essential keys to leading well in today's chaotic world. It strikes me that his emotionally agile approach is essential to maintaining good health and balance. We are in a battle, and often it's within ourselves!

Sometimes, it seems we go to battle every day, leading our teams and fighting our competition. In a wonderful way, Kevin delivers the map to peace and success for all who read this book and take action. There is a fitting use of military quotes leading the reader into each concept!

Kevin has delivered a leadership development piece containing wonderful, thoughtful therapy and specific actions for leaders. Take advantage of that rare combination. I'm excited to get this book into the hands of everyone on the team at Rose International and my family at home!"

—**Eric T. Token,** EVP Sales & Marketing,
Rose International, Inc.

"The book is engaging at all points . . . even when I felt like it was punching me in the gut. The analogies make it easy to digest. *The Emotionally Agile Leader* is about becoming the best version of yourself as a leader and serving your people through a relevant approach. It provides a play-by-play picture of what emotions to look for and what to do to make the best of them. This book also gives you an idea of how to harness and use those emotions to achieve goals. Be a lion. Kevin's insights will help you understand your value and responsibility as a leader. This book is applicable to anyone who wants to lead regardless of industry, tenure, or limitations."

—**Roger Cantu,** Network Infrastructure Lead,
TekSystems

"This book is both a thorough overview on leadership and a deep dive into individual components of being a successful and important leader. Because of that, it is valuable whether you choose to carefully read through it word for word or to skim through the pages looking for topics that stand out. Regardless of the approach, every reader will find something that resonates with their past experiences or, more importantly, something they can apply in their current experience. This is a handbook for recognizing what kind of leader you are and for identifying steps you can take to improve your approach, effectiveness, and ultimately your satisfaction as a leader."

—Dan L. DeVries, Contracts Engineer,
ExxonMobil Research and Engineering Company

"I thoroughly enjoyed this read! It is easy to follow, very informative, and caused me to think about myself as a leader and a person. This book imparts the keys that I can use in developing other leaders in the church and in other areas where I serve. *The Emotionally Agile Leader* is enlightening and encouraging. It is a joy to learn what actions can help or hinder a leader; Kevin shares ideas that every leader should aspire to connect with."

—Henry Sweeney,
Teacher and Associate Pastor

"From his original profound thesis to his final word, Kevin's concise, digestible text is packed with application—the most vital need for a leader. I have not read such a practical, useful, and engaging book on leadership for many years. As I read, I could feel Kevin painstakingly peeling back the veneer of my years filled with mediocre leadership practices. His insights initially made me uncomfortable, but his prescriptions for application made me aware of how to become a truly effective leader.

Using commonsense anecdotes and drawing from brief observations of some of history's most-recognized leaders, Kevin connects the enormous challenge facing leaders today (that is, remaining dynamically relevant and effective) with the crucial task of laying a reliable foundation of skills stressing the value of the person, not the profit."

—David G. Woods,
Dean, Virginia District Training Center,
Adjunct Instructor of Pastoral Ministries,
Nazarene Bible College

"Great read. Kevin has taken a vast amount of material and boiled it down to key points of application. Early in my career, I was floundering because my leaders were fixed on themselves. I needed someone to take the time to walk me through materials while developing an implementation plan. Kevin has provided an example of this in his book. I could follow the premise, apply the material through the examples, and laugh at my own failures as he shared some of his. The practical nature of applying emotional intelligence to leadership provides what I craved early in my career in education.

As I face the twilight of my career, Kevin reminded me to make sure that I leave the field of education and ministry better than I found it. He provides succinct and practical steps for me to engage in today, so tomorrow's leaders can advance. Thank you for the challenge, methodology, and focus on results."

—David A. Ruhman, PhD,
School Administrator, Union Grove Christian School

"This book takes a direct approach to leadership, cutting out some of the gray that we tend to live with. In doing so, Kevin raises the accountability factor for current leaders or people looking to become leaders. This book speaks to what leaders are experiencing; as companies constantly realign to meet client demands, leaders need the emotional intelligence to lead their teams. Leaders should be constantly learning and regularly requesting feedback from their staff and other leaders. *The Emotionally Agile Leader* can be a real call to action for those looking to take greater accountability personally and professionally."

—Arturo Odoms, Manager,
Human Resources, Black Knight Financial Services

"Kevin has delivered a timeless blueprint for those who struggle to cement a leadership legacy. The most meaningful way to impart success to others is to bring them into the idea generation process, which is precisely what this book does. The result is a multiplier effect that is immeasurable and applicable to any organization **and** family."

—**Ragan Shawell,**
Managing Director, Energy Vertical, DISYS

"Having been a captain both on ships and in business, I can honestly say that this book addresses the performance qualities necessary when your footing in this chaotic world is constantly changing. Have your basic skills solid (learning), keep your head about you (emotionally stable), and lead—don't manage, don't boss around, don't yell, and don't scream and shout; lead confidently and intentionally. Why do we want to lead this way? Because people depend on you to do so. They need their leader to maintain that firm yet flexible hand at the helm, making constant adjustments and corrections as needed. This book will help you to be that leader."

—**Keith R. Wahl,**
Owner, Made in Rhode Island

"In a world full of gray between leaders and followers, Kevin cuts through the fog, showing us that people matter most. And since people are different, the emotionally agile leader must seek first to understand, all the while being courageous enough to attack waves of conflict head on to minimize damage. Counterintuition is rampant in Kevin's philosophy, and for that, we are grateful."

—**Chad Mozingo,**
Men's Ministry Leader,
Former Professional Baseball Player

"My recent work environment has been chaotic as I transitioned to a new position. Reading this book was the one thing that helped me through without losing my mind while managing situations out of my control. As one who has been positively impacted by Kevin's writing, I can say emphatically that this book works. I read *Emotional Intelligence 2.0*, but Kevin's book provides a better way of applying the concepts. So far, it has given me tools that I will use in my current position and as I grow professionally."

—Alejandro Tortoriello,
Bio-Innovation Fellow and MD, Anderson Cancer Center

"What an easy and valuable read! Kevin has captured the essence of empathetic leadership like few others. Most authors bend the message to suit corporate America. Kevin brings real-life knowledge, experience, and wisdom to the reader, providing an entirely untainted view of what emotionally agile leaders should carry in their quivers as they move forward on their leadership journey. Kevin's ability to apply the right anecdotes and quotes at the right time is no less than exceptional. Well done."

—Sandy Marger,
Global Strategic Relationship Director, Deloitte and Touche

"As an avid reader, I marvel that Kevin was able to etch such an indelible picture of his message starting in the Introduction and resonating throughout this book. A must-read for any leader with a desire to grow!"

—Cody Rozier,
CEO, Zalemo

"I read *The Emotionally Agile Leader* straight through, and I found it not only interesting in prose and deliberate in content, but also insightful and inspiring. This book coaches you through each section with refreshing intentionality, using memorable stories to drive home the message with exceptional clarity. I found myself feeling proud that I had executed successfully in my leadership roles according to some of Kevin's precepts but then feeling regret that I hadn't been as successful in other areas of my leadership. Kevin's writing is easy to follow and complimentary to one's knowledge and experience; he excels at being instructive without being pedantic."

—Jack Boller,
Senior Solutions Consultant, LineDrive

THE
EMOTIONALLY
AGILE
LEADER

LIVING, LEARNING, AND LEADING
IN A CHAOTIC WORLD

KEVIN E. BOWSER

LUCIDBOOKS

The Emotionally Agile Leader
Living, Learning, and Leading in a Chaotic World

Copyright © 2018 by Kevin Bowser

Published by Lucid Books in Houston, TX
www.LucidBooksPublishing.com

ISBN-10: 1-63296-261-6
ISBN-13: 978-1-63296-261-4
eISBN-10: 1-63296-258-6
eISBN-13: 978-1-63296-258-4

Special Sales: Most Lucid Books titles are available in special quantity discounts. Custom imprinting or excerpting can also be done to fit special needs. Contact Lucid Books at Info@LucidBooksPublishing.com.

TABLE OF CONTENTS

Introduction   **1**

Introspective: **11**
Emotionally Agile Leaders Understand Their Emotions

Disciplined: **33**
Emotionally Agile Leaders Manage Their Emotions

Observant: **47**
Emotionally Agile Leaders Are Aware of Their Social Interactions

Influential: **63**
Emotionally Agile Leaders Manage Their Social Interactions

Proliferative: **71**
Emotionally Agile Leaders Create More Leaders

Conclusion: **87**
Becoming an Emotionally Agile Leader

Appendix: **91**
The Emotionally Agile Leader Methodology

Notes   **103**

Acknowledgments   **107**

INTRODUCTION

*I suppose leadership at one time meant muscles; but
today it means getting along with people.*
—Mahatma Gandhi

Consider the Rockhopper Penguin

Inspiration sometimes comes from unlikely sources.

I recently watched a documentary[1] about rockhopper penguins. It was about a group of very dedicated penguins who were trying, trying, and trying again to come ashore on one of the Falkland Islands to get to their breeding ground. With each attempt to reach the steep, rocky shore, a wave would come crashing in, sweeping the penguins off the narrow ledges and washing them back out to sea. Then, they would swim back toward the shore and begin their ascent up the rocky cliffs until another wave and then another knocked them back down.

Their urge to breed was their driving force, and they just kept trying and trying, again and again. Each time they were knocked off the cliffs, their little bodies—with a thick layer of fat under their skin and soft feathers on the outside—plunged into the surging surf, bounced around, and then popped back up. They refused to give up.

The penguins' persistence in relentlessly pursuing their goal is a great analogy for our leadership model. But there was another analogy as I watched more of the documentary. Suddenly, the penguins' persistence was not what was most notable. Instead, it was the way they handled adversity each time they were pounded by the waves.

These little penguins understood the rhythm of the waves, and they sensed when each big wave was about to hit. Milliseconds before it hit them, they pivoted and faced the oncoming wave. They literally turned and lowered their heads to let the wave hit them head on.

Why would they do such a thing? Because facing the wave created a smaller, more aerodynamic target for the wave. If the wave broadsided them, it would knock them back with a blunt force. However, when they turned and faced the wave head on, the pounding water flowed over them and around them. Then, the penguins quickly pivoted back and made their incremental progress up the cliff before the next wave was upon them.

Leadership is all about change and overcoming adversity. How do you deal with change and adversity? Do they hit you broadside? Or do you turn and face them head on? Like the penguins, we cannot stop the waves from crashing into us. But we can change the angle at which they hit us. We can choose to turn, face the waves head on, and lean into them so they have a smaller target.

It is amazing what a little rockhopper penguin can teach us about becoming an Emotionally Agile Leader.

My Hypothesis

I am not afraid of an army of lions led by a sheep;
I am afraid of an army of sheep led by a lion.
—Alexander the Great

Emotional intelligence (EI) alone is not enough to make someone a great leader. To become great leaders, we must develop the ability to adapt to ever-changing situations and become agile in our leadership. We must be able to practically apply the principles of emotional intelligence to our daily lives. It is this agile application that moves us from simple intelligence to emotional wisdom.

What Is Emotional Intelligence?

Let's first look at a high-level summary of emotional intelligence. By now, many of you have read the book *Emotional Intelligence 2.0* by Travis Bradberry and Jean Greaves.[2] Their discussion of emotional intelligence is an important study. But for the purpose of this book, let's look at a succinct definition of EI. The quick answer is to say that there are four components of emotional intelligence that best define it. The first two are about yourself, while the other two concern those around you.

Self-Consciousness (Being Aware of Your Own Emotions)

Knowing yourself and being conscious of your emotions is the first component of emotional intelligence. Becoming aware of yourself involves observing your own emotions, distinguishing your reactions, and then knowing what kind of emotions you are experiencing. When you know your own feelings and emotions and how they shape your attitude and actions, you can better understand yourself, so your self-esteem and conviction can grow.

Self-Control (Managing Your Own Emotions)

Being able to control or manage your own emotions is the second component of emotional intelligence. Knowing your emotions is a good start, but learning how to manage them should follow. Properly managing your impulses and compulsive behaviors allows you to be on top of every situation. Most people have a commitment problem because they first have an emotion problem. If you can keep your emotions in check most of the time, you can finish your obligations, follow through on your responsibilities, and deliver on your promises. You will also become more proactive in everything you do and adapt to change more easily. This component of EI is applicable not only at work but also in your personal life dealing with family and friends.

Sensitivity (Being Aware of the Emotions of Others)

The third component of emotional intelligence is being sensitive to the emotions of others. This aspect is about understanding others and putting yourself in their position without being emotionally affected by it. It also means identifying the exact emotional needs of a person, quickly grasping poignant cues, making others feel comfortable with your presence, and knowing when to take advantage of group emotions. If you are able to understand, sympathize with, and show compassion to the people around you, you will be able to manage your relationships with them well, which brings us to the final component.

Sociability (Managing Your Relationships with Others)

The fourth and final component of emotional intelligence is sociability. The first three aspects actually conclude with this one. Sociability involves managing all life's relationships and making them more fruitful. Your ultimate aim in developing emotional intelligence should be to become more relatable, which involves various kinds of skills, including communication skills and people skills, which we will look at in the rest of this book. Sociability also includes harnessing teamwork in a group and being able to handle conflicts and disagreements.

But what good is all this knowledge if it has no practical value? My hypothesis is that knowledge is absolutely worthless unless you can put it into action and contribute to your overall success as a leader.

The Emotionally Agile Leader

The Problem

"No plan survives first contact with the enemy." This saying gained great notoriety in the early days of the Iraq War and has been attributed to everyone from General George Patton to Will Rogers. But it actually comes from Helmuth Von Moltke, a Prussian general and great military tactician. Here is what he said: "No plan of operations extends with any certainty beyond the first contact with the main hostile force."[3]

Both the original quote and the pithier shortened version demonstrate the need for a leader to be emotionally agile. Leaders must have the ability to pivot as the "plan of operations extends . . . beyond the first contact."

It seems that if a little penguin can do something so extraordinary when faced with pounding waves, then certainly you and I should be able to handle the challenges of leadership. Unfortunately, leadership is not that simple. Many of the world's problems and the issues that organizations, businesses, and people face every day can seem intractable and unsolvable. It is the extreme variability of leadership challenges that proves to be the most problematic.

The Solution

The solution lies within the application of the emotional intelligence principles of which so many of us have become aware in recent days. But before we dive into emotional agility, let's take a quick look at a similar leadership technique in order to understand the distinction.

In 2009, leadership consultants Ronald Heifetz, Alexander Grashow, and Marty Linsky discussed a new way to lead the charge to change in their book *The Practice of Adaptive Leadership*. The book calls for leaders to move beyond the approaches and leadership paradigms of the past and move toward embracing new skills and attitudes to guide their organizations in the twenty-first century.[4] Adaptive leadership combines established ways of leading with new skills and new perspectives to deal with unprecedented challenges and a pace of change that can be dizzying.

So adaptive leadership is the way to go, right? Not so fast. Adaptive leadership is fundamentally about how an individual leader addresses the issue of change management within an organization. For example, adaptive leadership has been used by a variety of change management consultants out there. Companies such as Accenture and KPMG employ entire armies of consultants who can parachute into an organization and help it make significant changes.

But agile leadership is more concerned with people (primarily) and the processes (secondarily) that will be affected by the change. It is in this realm that a leader's understanding and firm grasp of emotional intelligence really pay off for both the leader and the organization.

Perhaps a better way to look at this is to look at the difference between *adaptive* and *agile* by using a nautical analogy. Adaptive does, indeed, indicate change. But the change can be imperceptibly slow. It can be evolutionary, not revolutionary. Or it can be like a giant battleship or aircraft carrier that must have the ability to turn and maneuver. And they do. They just can't do it fast. It takes time and distance to turn around a giant ship.

Contrast that with the Swift Boats used in the Vietnam War. They were small shallow-draft vessels used to patrol the coastal and inland waterways of the Mekong Delta. As their name indicates, they were small, fast, and highly maneuverable. With a small counterintelligence force, they could get in and out of a dangerous situation where larger craft could not even enter. And they could do it while acting as an offensive or defensive force. They exemplify the concept of agility, and they are a stark contrast to being merely adaptive.

As Emotionally Agile Leaders, we must assess how we implement change, address the impact of the change, and help guide people through the losses (real or imagined) that they feel as a result of the change process. We must learn to discern between technical and agility issues.

Technical issues are the kind you can plug into a Microsoft or Primavera project plan. These issues are about steps, timing, and identifying the items on the critical path to a successful implementation. Documentation and approvals are technical items.

Agility issues are the kind you experience on an emotional level. They are about *who* will be affected and not *what* the outcome will be once implemented. Agility issues will always impact the technical issues. They will address the pace of the change so the organization can absorb and process how life will be different post-change.

This is the crux of agile leadership. For example, in a merger or acquisition, grafting together two firms' computer environments is actually a technical job. A team of certified systems or software engineers can handle that task. However, figuring out how to do it and discovering the synergies between each company's culture and values are agile leadership challenges that require a healthy understanding of the role that emotions and emotional intelligence play in the ultimate success of the merger.

Agile leadership is built on the foundation of high degrees of emotional intelligence. Finding a way to bring convergent organizations and teams together while keeping the enthusiasm, knowledge, wisdom, values, and energy that created the original organization is crucial to finding new ways of leading and facing the new challenges that come our way on a daily basis. Agile leadership happens when we communicate and connect on a level that is not solely based on facts and data.

And here is one additional agile leadership principle. People don't learn by staring in the mirror. They learn by engaging with others. Emotionally Agile Leaders welcome different viewpoints and resolve conflicts across organizational and individual boundaries. But conflict is inevitable. And change is disruptive. Emotionally Agile Leaders must be willing to go the extra mile and prepare for and offset the emotional reactions that their followers will experience.

To summarize, let's create a working definition of an Emotionally Agile Leader. The Emotionally Agile Leader takes the awareness and knowledge of Emotional Intelligence and applies those skills, along with the awareness of themselves and of others, to adapt to the ever-changing leadership landscape. Emotionally Agile Leaders recognize that they cannot change the way the waves of emotion crash upon the shores of their situations. Emotionally Agile Leaders change the way they face those crashing waves.

Before exploring ways to become more emotionally agile in our leadership, we must first harness the power of asking questions. Most of the questions we ask will be internally focused. Consider the following overarching question as we move forward: What does an Emotionally Agile Leader look like in each dynamic of the EI quadrant?

The EI quadrant is a graphic representation of the work by Bradberry and Greaves in an attempt to define the *something* that each of us has within us that is intangible. It is what affects how we manage our own behavior, attempt to influence others' behaviors, navigate social interactions, and make personal decisions that achieve positive results in the culture around us. Bradberry represents these concepts by showing that emotional intelligence is made up of four core skills: self-awareness, self-management, social awareness, and relationship management. These, in turn, correlate to two primary competencies: personal competence and social competence.[5]

I will demonstrate in the coming pages the way this quadrant correlates to leadership and the emotional agility that defines great leaders. I would modify Bradberry's model of the EI quadrant as shown on page 10.

Agile leadership starts with our own perspective. It starts with our perspective on people. It causes us to ask some reflective questions such as these: Do I value those around me? Am I able to truly feel what they feel? In other words, am I

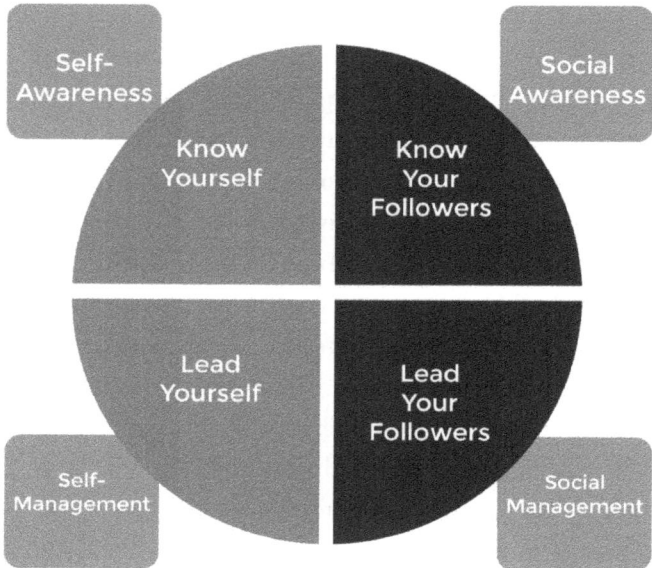

empathetic? Can I adapt and become agile as each person and situation warrants?

What Kind of Leader Are You?

The impetus behind the writing of this book is to provide practical approaches to agile leadership. Do you see a need for agile leadership in your organization? Do you see yourself as an Emotionally Agile Leader? And if not, do you see yourself developing the skills to become one? The bottom line is that leaders need to understand the importance of being agile. What's more, leaders need to be able to instill the necessary processes and tools into an entire organization, so it will be comfortable in the midst of change as these processes and tools become part of the organization's DNA. Stay with me through the coming pages, and we will explore agility in much greater depth.

INTROSPECTIVE

Emotionally Agile Leaders
Understand Their Emotions

*If you know the enemy and know yourself you need
not fear the results of a hundred battles.*

—Sun Tzu

In August 1902, Rafford Pyke wrote an article called "What Men Like in Men." (In 1902, no one would think twice about a title worded this way.) Pyke explained this:

> The typical man is curiously deficient in a capacity for self-analysis. He seldom devotes any serious thought to the origin of his opinions, the determining factor in his judgments, the ultimate source of his desires, or the hidden mainsprings of his motives. In all that relates to the external and material world he observes shrewdly, reasons logically, and acts effectively; but question him as to the phenomena of the inner world—the world of his own Ego—and he is dazed and helpless.[1]

Here is the problem. Many leaders suffer from extreme introspection aversion. We are unwilling to take an objective look at ourselves and our leadership style. We fail to do the work to understand ourselves. Introspection is a powerful leadership tool, but we often neglect to use it.

But Emotionally Agile Leaders must be introspective. They should know their strengths and weaknesses better than anyone. How do they accomplish this? They continually work to increase their self-awareness. They request feedback from others about the impressions they make on other people and the wake they create with their decisions.

When you ask yourself what behaviors hold you and your team back, you can recalibrate your leadership style for the better. This pursuit of self-awareness is the essence of emotional intelligence and emotional agility as it relates to leadership. When you give your staff the freedom and the space to tell you the hard truths, without fear of repercussion, you'll get valuable perspectives of yourself and make a giant leap forward in maturing as a leader.

In this first section, we'll look at how leaders can strengthen their level of introspection.

What Should the Emotionally Agile Leader Learn?

The person who strives to become an Emotionally Agile Leader must begin by looking inward. Before we can start changing our actions to become more effective leaders and mentors, we have to first begin with ourselves and find out what our patterns are and why we fall into those patterns. We have to learn and accept our strengths and our weaknesses and become aware of how we are affecting others. Real leaders do not blame others for why they aren't successful as leaders. Instead, they learn more about themselves in order to understand how they impact other people. Once you know how you come across to others, you can begin to change how you interact with them. You must have this awareness before you can figure out how to lead well and influence others.

The Emotionally Agile Leader knows that orthodoxy leads to orthopraxy. In other words, knowing leads to doing. The more you understand yourself, the better you understand the areas in which you need to grow. In this case, knowing involves self-knowledge and self-awareness.

Understanding ourselves is also where agility comes into play. Leaders have to understand the root of their emotional responses so they can pinpoint emotions that are affecting them negatively and learn to quickly adapt to challenges they face throughout the day. Recognizing negative emotions you suffer from can help you grow and thrive in the workplace instead of falling prey to weaknesses. As we begin to learn about ourselves, let's look at some of the most common emotions that can negatively affect leaders.

Paul Ekman is an American psychologist and professor emeritus at the University of California, San Francisco. He identified six basic emotions from which all others stem. He claims that anger, disgust, fear, happiness, sadness, and surprise are the basis for all emotional expressions. Robert Plutchik, professor emeritus at the Albert Einstein College of Medicine, identified eight emotions. He grouped them into four pairs that represent polar opposites. Those pairs are joy-sadness, anger-fear, trust-distrust, and surprise-anticipation.[2]

My observations and experiences have pointed to some variation within these core emotions as described in many academic writings. For instance, I have not found disgust to be particularly prevalent from a leadership perspective, but I have found jealousy to be a core emotion that affects leaders and their leadership endeavors.

The real key for Emotionally Agile Leaders is to identify the core emotions within themselves so they can go from understanding to managing those core emotions. The principle they must live by is this: You can't work on what you can't identify.

Let's look at the core emotions that can significantly affect leaders.

Anger

Anger is a powerful emotion—even emotionally strong, mature leaders still get angry. Anger can be harnessed for positive results, but if not controlled, it can destroy our relationships in the workplace and our effectiveness as leaders. What are the roots of anger?

Unmet or Unrealistic Expectations

One common root of anger is having set expectations that are not fulfilled. Maybe we've had experiences in other settings or contexts, and we expect to have the same experience in the current context. We also may not have an accurate assessment of the current situation and have thus created unrealistic outcomes. In other words, when a team is assigned an arbitrary deadline and the timeline of the project should be double the allotted time, it is not very realistic to expect success for that project.

Anger can have severe consequences. It creates lack of trust from employees and brings about broken relationships. It also creates a lack of communication due to fear among employees and even peers. Anger creates a failure to see situations objectively and make sound decisions.

Disappointment

Another root cause of anger is disappointment. We are often disappointed because those around us did not act the way we had hoped they would. While that might seem similar to the discussion about expectations, it's actually different because disappointment may occur regardless of whether the situation warrants it or not. In other words, we can experience disappointment whether our expectations are reasonable or unreasonable. In fact, our disappointment tends to be much greater when the person who causes the disappointment has the necessary skills to accomplish what we expected of them but fail to follow through. We feel disappointed with their results and usually with them as well. We can also be disappointed in ourselves for the same reason. Perhaps we just didn't try hard enough, or perhaps we procrastinated and didn't have time to do our best with the project.

Disappointment with ourselves and other people can then turn into anger. We're angry at people for not working hard, we're angry at ourselves for wasting time, or maybe we blame other people for the disappointing results when deep down we know the result was our fault. Differentiating and separating our disappointment from the act and the actor requires high levels of maturity and emotional intelligence.

What are the consequences of our disappointment? Disappointment can lead to broken relationships along with broken communication due to fear among employees and peers. It can also cause a failure to see situations objectively and make sound decisions. Recognizing trends of disappointment is vital in strengthening our relationships in the workplace.

Lost Opportunities

Lost opportunities can be another significant source of anger for leaders. We may have missed a chance to accomplish something special, and the opportunity will never come around again. That situation is at the root of many of my own emotions. Lost opportunities haunt me and cause me to feel intense emotions of loss, sadness, anger, and frustration.

Like many in my generation, I was raised with this maxim: You never get a second opportunity to make a good first impression. Did you catch the word that haunts me? It's that word *never*. Never is a very long time. To think that I would have one chance and one chance only at something can be almost paralyzing at times. What if I mess up? What if my first impression is not positive? I will never be able to recover from that first impression and turn things around.

From a more mature perspective, the reality is that life does offer second chances. I can even turn around a bad first impression. However, the thought of having one chance and one chance only and missing that opportunity still looms large in my psyche.

But giving into anger because of lost opportunities leads to harmful effects for leaders. We can develop a paralyzing fear of doing anything at all in case something goes wrong and causes us to waste an opportunity. The fear prevents us from even trying. We can also begin to take on an overly analytical approach to everything in life. Instead of trusting our instincts, we try to look at each situation from every possible angle before we make a move. And as a result, the thing we fear the most—missing an opportunity—happens because of our lack of action.

Missed Deadlines

Recently, I missed a significant deadline at work. I had been assigned some deliverables by very senior executives in my organization. But I wasn't at the meeting where these tasks were assigned, and as a result, I had an unclear picture of my responsibilities.

I worked diligently on the assignment. About a week and a half before the deadline, I was reviewing my progress with my boss in a one-on-one session in her office and reported that I had nearly completed the assignment and would be ready by the end of the month's deadline. As I began to describe my deliverable, her eyes grew wide. What I had produced was not what she was expecting and had agreed to. There was much more to the assignment than I had realized. Much more detailed research needed to be done, and that research would take about six more weeks to accomplish. Had I understood that from the beginning, I would have had plenty of time to accomplish the assignment. But now I would miss the deadline.

Thankfully, the failure wasn't fatal. Of course, my boss, colleagues, and I were disappointed, but we were able to quickly regroup and determine that the deadline was arbitrary to begin with. What's more, we hadn't clearly communicated with one another, so we learned more about each other's communication styles and how each of us used a different set of base assumptions.

When encountering missed deadlines, anger is an easy emotion to jump to. We often don't pause to consider the workload of our employees or the events that went wrong. In other words, was there a catastrophic event that impacted the deadline in an unforeseeable manner? We also do not consider that we may have been poor planners and did not adequately prepare for the approaching deadline.

If we react with anger when deadlines are missed, what are the potential consequences? The results of the anger generated within our emotional self and the anger felt by our followers are substantial. Such anger can fracture longstanding relationships and inhibit the growth of developing relationships.

Unexpected Results

Half of my time is spent in an engineering environment. Engineers tend to build everything from mathematical calculations. Their motto is this: If you can't do it in an Excel spreadsheet, it isn't worth doing. They love that mathematics is defined. If you add a column of numbers today and then add that same column of numbers in a year or a thousand years, you'll get the same result. Numbers do not waver. In this environment, an unexpected result can almost cause panic.

The other part of my time is spent working with nonprofit organizations. These are typically not led by engineers. They are more often led by visionaries and charismatic leaders. The very thought of predicting a result is foreign to them. They would rarely sit down and develop a what-if scenario. The thought of contingencies and plan B is far from their minds.

Yet both groups have expectations. The engineers have their expectations documented, and the visionaries don't. But both groups have them, and both groups can have similar emotional responses to any unexpected results.

There is a great line from the movie *Forrest Gump* that comes to mind here. The lead character, Forrest Gump (played by Tom Hanks), said, "My momma always said life was like a box of chocolates. You never know what you're gonna get."[3] Forrest's mother was right. We need to be prepared for the possibility that the piece we bite into has the dreaded creamy orange filling instead of the caramel we were expecting.

But when we have planned and prepared for X only to have Y happen, Emotionally Agile Leaders know how to handle that situation, and they do not panic. Instead, they go back to the starting line and start over. Or they might take the unexpected results and modify them so they fit the purpose.

You must be prepared for the possibility of an unexpected result. An Emotionally Agile Leader is mentally and emotionally ready for life's curve balls.

What does anger due to unexpected results affect? Just like the discussion on missed deadlines, the anger generated when we encounter unexpected results can lead to an overall lack of trust toward the people who produced the unexpected results. This anger will erode a leader's confidence in their team and make team members fear bringing anything unexpected to the leader.

Lack of Loyalty
The final significant cause of anger is lack of loyalty. The reality of life in the workplace today is that there seems to be a larger population of workers who are not loyal to the organization versus those who are loyal. And much of the research on employee transition shows that employees leave a boss more often than they leave a company.[4] This is a sobering thought for leaders.

Encountering disloyalty in our employees can be very disheartening and lead to deep anger. We feel betrayed and frustrated and begin to lose trust in our team. However, loyalty is a complex matter. What I perceive as a lack of loyalty can often just be the natural questioning of my leadership by some people around me. People need to understand why we're doing what we are doing. Many times, we want to take routine questions and even routine challenges to our leadership as an attack upon us rooted in a lack of loyalty. Or perhaps I perceive disloyalty because of my insecurity or a false perspective. And it is that complexity and our own emotional agility that can cause us to misinterpret whether or not someone is disloyal.

What are the consequences of anger toward perceived disloyalty? The most obvious consequence is turnover within an organization. If your employees feel you are bitter toward past workers or do not trust their loyalty, they can easily become discouraged. They feel hopeless about impressing you and about gaining your trust because they know they're working hard and don't know what else to do to earn your trust. Establishing a clear understanding of loyalty among your followers, as well as your reaction to disloyalty, is vital to becoming an Emotionally Agile Leader.

Fear

Why do leaders become afraid? Fear can creep in because leaders feel like they've lost control of a situation. It can be rooted in self-doubt and lack of confidence. Fear can also overtake us because we did not adequately prepare. (Do you remember the fear of being called on by a teacher when you hadn't read the homework chapter the night before?) Let's discuss some of the typical causes of fear for leaders.

Loss of Control

Rudyard Kipling started his poem "If" like this: "If you can keep your head when all about you are losing theirs and blaming it on you."[5] What aspect of your workplace is out of control? Is it the situation that is out of control, or is it those around you? Or are you out of control? Let's assume that you have correctly evaluated the situation and that things are, in fact, out of control. How did the situation get to that point? Where did you lose control? One of the things that the Emotionally Agile Leader understands is that there are at least two types of situations out there. There are those that I *can* control. And there are those that I *cannot*. Emotionally Agile Leaders understand that distinction and focus most, if not all, their energy on those situations that can be controlled and then dismiss those that cannot be controlled after a quick triage. All their remaining energy then flows toward the situations that can be controlled.

Further triage can even point Emotionally Agile Leaders to the level of effort needed to create control in every situation. For instance, if you are leading a project team with a fixed budget and no contingency, then expending emotional energy on trying to boost the budget will not be productive. Consider reducing the scope instead. I may not be able to control the income or revenue, but I can control the expenses. Emotionally Agile Leaders follow that initial triage with a further quick analysis so they can focus on the things that bring about the greatest return on the investment of their time, talents, and treasures.

What are the consequences of fear caused by loss of control? The effects on leaders can be debilitating. Fear of losing control ranks right up there with fear of speaking in public. We can often avoid the need to speak in public, but the fear of losing control seeps into our consciousness and subconsciousness without always having a cause-and-effect connection. Leaders who suffer from this fear tend to become more and more withdrawn and inwardly focused. That, in turn, begins to affect them externally because they abandon relationships and responsibilities they cannot control and instead seek to control the only thing they can control: themselves.

Another way we manifest fear from losing control is to supervise those around us ever more tightly. In business settings, that results in micromanaging. When a leader has experienced and capable followers, micromanaging has a huge negative impact on the team and reduces productivity. The team is so busy worrying about what their leader will think, say, or do that they have no time for creativity and innovation—two things so desperately needed in organizations.

Leaders with a bent toward perfectionism are some of the most susceptible to feelings of loss of control. The Emotionally Agile Leader must become comfortable with a certain amount of uncertainty and be willing to let their followers achieve their potential.

Self-Doubt

Why do we doubt ourselves? Many of us have struggled with self-doubt our entire lives, and at times, leaders struggle more with self-doubt. Consider how we viewed ourselves as children and how those who had a real influence over us viewed us. Were we given the appropriate amount of encouragement and praise for our efforts and outcomes? Did key people in our lives fail to encourage us? Did they plant seeds of insecurity? Or does our self-doubt stem from current situations when we face a new or unexpected challenge?

Self-doubt is usually manifested in several ways. One is the inability to give yourself a little credit for doing something right. Another is that sometimes you feel like a poser. And sometimes you have a soundtrack playing in your head from your childhood and can't hear any other message. We tend to record the things that people have said to us over the years. Many of us remember exactly what was said and how it made us feel as if it were yesterday.

But all these manifestations allow fear to creep into our minds and into how we interact with others. Here again is where emotions collide. Self-doubt is permanently connected to the emotion of fear. And if it's not exactly fear you feel, then maybe it is fear's cousin—dread. Dread is the emotion of great apprehension about something or someone. It is different from fear in that fear is often associated with the unknown, while dread is that negative emotion we feel when we anticipate something very unpleasant we have experienced before.

Fear and dread in the lives of leaders will usually have a direct effect on their workplace. What does our team hear from us when the stress level is high? Is it a diatribe? Is it the same type of soundtrack you might be playing in your head? If it is, then understand that this soundtrack sticks in people's minds just like the song "Let It Go" from the movie *Frozen*. Once you hear that song, you just can't get it out of your head, right?

As leaders, it is important to remember the role we play in our followers' lives. In many work situations, we spend more time with our workmates than we do with our families. Projects have deadlines, and deadlines cause stress. How we perform, how we communicate, and how we respond to those around us have a lot to do with what those relationships will become over time. What does our team hear from us when things are going well? What do they hear from us when things are not going so well? How do we deliver a message under each of those circumstances?

We all know the basic leadership principle that says to praise publicly and correct privately. Let your words that are said in public be affirming words that build your team up. Don't seek to criticize in public. There is a time and a place for that. We need to be sure that our expectations for performance are, indeed, appropriate to our team members' skill levels and realistically achievable.

Remember, your words of praise will be indelibly recorded on the soundtrack of their minds. Unfortunately, so will the things we say that wreck our followers' confidence and self-esteem. Let's be the kind of leader that our team wants to follow, not the kind of leader that yells orders and then is negative about the way they are followed. When you do that, you are creating a soundtrack in their minds that is hard to erase or record over.

The consequences of our endless loop of negative messages and self-doubt can be debilitating, and the consequences on our followers will be the same. Why would their psyche respond any differently than our own under the same stimulus?

Lack of Preparation

Consider for a moment Humpty Dumpty, that character from our childhood nursery rhymes. Obviously, Humpty Dumpty possessed a certain amount of planning and preparation skills. Otherwise, how would he have gotten his rather portly, fragile self perched atop that wall in the first place? But that is where the planning seems to have stopped. Apparently, he had not contemplated what would happen if he lost his balance, if there was a sudden gust of wind, or if some nefarious character from another nursery rhyme pushed him off the wall. (I bet it was Simple Simon or maybe even Jack Horner who did it.)

Why are we unprepared? Perhaps we did not plan appropriately. We may not have had adequate resources. It is even possible that we underestimated the task from the very beginning. Regardless of the reason, we fear that our lack of preparation will be exposed, and we fear the consequences that exposure will bring.

Everyone remembers that feeling of showing up at school in the morning and realizing there is a test for which you did not study. That feeling is rooted in fear—fear of failure, fear of being the only one to not do well since everyone else studied the night before, and fear of the consequences when grades are posted. These are just a few examples of the kind of fear associated with lack of preparation.

Most leaders have skills in basic planning and preparation. But Emotionally Agile Leaders are also skilled in the tasks of planning and preparation to grow and increase their leadership scope and influence. Properly prepared leaders exude confidence. And confidence draws more followers, thus increasing their scope and influence. That builds the leader.

Since Emotionally Agile Leaders are more self-aware and socially aware, they build certain things into their planning. Perhaps in meetings, they allow more time for discovery and brainstorming on the front end because some people take a long time to warm up and begin to contribute in a group setting. Maybe they plan extra team recognition events since some people need that for their own sense of purpose and a feeling that their contributions are noticed and valued. That builds the followers and the organization. All these planning activities have their genesis in the planning skills of an Emotionally Agile Leader.

If you love failure, then simply do nothing and do not prepare. But make no mistake, fear will result from a lack of planning and preparation.

Jealousy

Why do leaders become jealous? Leaders can, of course, become jealous when they want what they cannot have or want what rightfully belongs to someone else. Jealousy is rooted in trust—or actually distrust. That distrust can be toward someone else, or it can be distrust of ourselves.

Distrust of others comes from an erosion of the trust of those who have done something to make us ponder our motivation. Did they have their own best interest at heart and therefore place themselves above the team and the organization? If so, then we become jealous of them.

Distrust of ourselves comes from knowing our own weaknesses (self-awareness) but having no confidence in our ability to control them (self-management). We then allow that emotion to turn into jealousy when we see others (social-awareness) who have those same weaknesses yet seem to be overcoming them (self-management).

Comparison

Playing the comparison game is always dangerous. We like to point to that one person we know who has what we don't have. We compare ourselves to that person and ask: Why can't I be like them?

Comparison is rooted in trust. I do not trust the truth that if I work hard and work with integrity I will usually compare favorably with my peers. Judging ourselves by our motivations and desires can be very tempting. We feel like we are working as hard as the next person, yet our careers have taken different trajectories. We lack the self-awareness to realize we have taken shortcuts while others are putting in the hours and working harder than we are. Of course, life is not always fair. Sometimes, we are doing all the right things and still don't achieve the results we want.

What are the consequences of falling prey to comparison and jealousy? Comparison affects our contentment. As I write this section, I find myself in Bangalore, India, where comparisons take on a much different set of observations. Every morning on my way to the office, I see untold numbers of people with whom I would come out favorable if I chose to compare myself to them. But we usually don't compare ourselves to those less fortunate than we are. It's more common to compare ourselves to one person who has something we do not have. I tend to compare what I do not have to what someone else seems to have. That comparison leaves me feeling lacking and wanting and quickly leads to feelings of jealousy. Any leader living with these emotions will slowly become a poison in the workplace.

Discontentment

Similar to the previous point, discontentment in general leads to jealousy. Am I always in need of one more thing to make me satisfied about the company? Do I need that senior leader to approve my work and acknowledge me publicly? Perhaps I see others receiving recognition, and the more they receive and the less I receive, the greater my discontentment level. Discontentment is a breeding ground for jealousy and many other negative emotions.

Projection

Projection is the act of viewing a situation and transmitting our feelings about it onto someone else. Most often, we are not aware that we are doing this. Instead, we feel justified in our anger or jealousy toward the other person when, in fact, it is our own behavior or feelings that are at the root of the jealousy.

The classic example often used to explain projection is the husband who feels a strong sense of attraction to a woman who is not his wife. His inner values tell him that is wrong. But rather than owning up to those feelings and working on his marriage, he projects his feelings onto his wife and accuses her of being unfaithful.

What are the consequences of projection? Projecting feelings of jealousy can drive a wedge between individuals and lead to increased feelings of anger and hostility. Hostility then feeds our negative emotions and makes it easier for us to experience stronger negative feelings and justify the wedge that now exists between us.

Protection

Another root of jealousy is protection. Protection as it relates to leadership means guarding the interests we have in advancing our leadership position or in defending against negative self-views that can be self-defeating.

First, what are we protecting? Most often, it is our own self-interests. High on the list of things we often protect is our ego. Unhealthy protection mechanisms include feelings such as denial, regression, repression, and sometimes acting out in negative ways. What is deemed to be healthy protection may include sublimation and compensation. However, both of those psychological terms have unhealthy aspects when carried to an extreme or when they remain unresolved for an extended period of time. I am not a psychologist, so I will not delve deeply into those terms. But there is a wealth of emotional and psychological help for those who would like to seek it.

What does protection affect? Protection is a fight-or-flight emotion. It can cause us to examine a situation or a relationship to much greater depths in order to determine if we want or need to be part of it on a long-term basis. In other words, do I stay and fight for the relationship or situation, or do I take flight and remove myself from what could be a harmful situation?

As much as this point is about self-protection, it is also about protecting others. Here is the tie to jealousy. We experience jealousy when we are denied the ability to protect someone or something that we feel needs protection. We become jealous of the protector.

Competition

Competition can be healthy and motivational, but not all competition is positive. We should not have to feel as though we are competing for the love of our family members, because competition means there is a winner and a loser. If I am the loser, I can become jealous of the winner, especially when they win much more often than I do.

What are the consequences? Jealousy places an unhealthy lens over competition. We view every activity as a win-or-lose situation. Competition affects our energy level and the focus of our attention. Instead of competing for attention with the object of our jealousy, why not focus on what differentiates us and our leadership abilities from the run-of-the-mill variety that is so prevalent? One of the guys in my circle of influence often says that there are riches in the niches. He means that there is great value in being uncommon. Celebrate the difference, and make the most of its positive potential.

Pride and Ego

Pride and ego are at the root of the downfall of many leaders. Whether we begin to believe our own so-called press releases or just have an unhealthy ego, the end result can be disastrous for leaders as they become more and more disconnected from their followers.

Why do leaders often begin to develop an unhealthy view of themselves? It is often because certain levels of influence and power come with leadership roles. And as emotional intelligence reminds us, we must know and understand ourselves fully and accurately, and then we must manage or control ourselves in order to become more emotionally intelligent. Is our pride caused by an unrealistic view of ourselves? Are we unable to see ourselves as those around us do? Or are we just choosing to be ignorant of how we come across?

The root of pride is found in its definitions—absorbed in oneself, boastful, conceited, narcissistic, self-absorbed, self-centered, self-important, self-interested, self-seeking, selfish, and vain. None of these seem to reflect a very high level of self-awareness and self-management, do they? In fact, they are quite the opposite.

What are the effects of pride? One effect is that leaders fail to serve their followers and those around them. That damages not only their relationships with their followers but also their work.

Let me provide an example from a recent business trip. It was the last night of my stay at the very luxurious Ritz-Carlton in Kuala Lumpur, Malaysia. Apparently, someone had alerted the general manager that I would be leaving very early the following morning. So he came to my dinner table in the dining room to introduce himself and say thank you for my extended stay (I had been at the hotel for three and a half weeks.) Soon after our brief discussion, I saw an extraordinary example of servant leadership.

A woman walking through the lobby was struggling with a large balloon bouquet and a suitcase. There were several other staff members in the vicinity who probably saw her. But the general manager did something that has stuck with me ever since. He graciously walked over to her, picked up her bag, and carried it to the bell captain while she completed her checkout routine.

He could have snapped his finger and had one of the junior hospitality staff take the bag. He could have very subtly caught the eye of one of them and asked them to do the menial task of carrying her bag. After all, he was the most senior person and outranked everyone else on the staff. His place was at the top. I wonder if he started his hotel career as a bellboy. I wonder if he ever thinks of those early days.

My guess is that he has not forgotten his more humble beginnings. My guess is that he has always had a servant's heart. My guess is that his focus on the patrons of the places he has worked has been what has propelled his career. My guess is that he has never lost sight of the customer.

What about you? What is your place? Do you know it? Are you in a place where you think you are above certain tasks? If so, be careful. You just might lose your place to someone who is still willing to carry a bag.

I said at the beginning of this section that pride and ego are at the root of the downfall of many leaders. Perhaps it is in the nonprofit world that we often see the glaring effects of these disasters. Of course, they occur in the commercial and academic worlds, but it seems to be a greater disaster for nonprofits (churches, charities, and philanthropic organizations) that should somehow be exempt from the negative consequences or oversized pride and ego.

An unhealthy level of pride is as hard to recognize in ourselves as it is easy to recognize in others. Let me take a moment to urge you to seek out the input or feedback from people you trust to help you gauge the level of pride you have for yourself or your leadership efforts. Then, take that feedback and seek the tools to help you develop a healthier, more humble level of pride.

DISCIPLINED

Emotionally Agile Leaders
Manage Their Emotions

I cannot trust a man to control others who cannot control himself.
—General Robert E. Lee

The Emotionally Agile Leader is self-disciplined. In the last section, we read about the importance of increasing our self-awareness. We saw that Emotionally Agile Leaders must learn what emotions are hindering them in their leadership.

But the work doesn't stop there. It is now time to take action. You now understand more about yourself. But as important as awareness—especially self-awareness—is to leaders, awareness alone is not sufficient and will not make you a better leader. The next building block is to take that awareness and build a plan to actually *do* something to grow in the areas where you are weak. That is, it's time to build self-discipline.

Self-discipline is at the root, or at least very near the root, of any successful leader. Leading by the seat of your pants without any planning or forethought will work occasionally. But self-discipline creates a structured approach to leadership and allows you to employ a repeatable process. That may seem at odds with the message of this book, which teaches the need for agility in leadership. But the concepts of self-control and self-discipline in no way contradict the need to be agile.

We can boil down self-discipline to this definition: the willingness to do what you know you need to do, even though you don't feel like it.

There it is. Did you catch it? You do something even though you don't feel like it. In fact, that may be one of the behaviors that separates leaders into two groups: the successful and the unsuccessful. Successful leaders do the right thing regardless of how they feel in the moment. As we've heard so often, the difference between winners and losers is that losers wait to feel good about a decision, and winners make a decision and wait to feel good about it later.

Even poor leaders can choose action when it is easy and enjoyable or when they feel like it. That is easy. But doing activities that are hard or unpleasant marks the difference between a leader with self-discipline and a leader without it.

Let's look at what the Emotionally Agile Leader should learn as he or she seeks to take self-awareness and put it into tangible action.

What Should the Emotionally Agile Leader Learn?

Show me the man you honor, and I will
know what kind of man you are.
—Thomas John Carlisle

Triggers

One of the skills that Emotionally Agile Leaders need to develop is the ability to identify the triggers that affect us on an emotional level. From time to time, I have the opportunity to speak to young leaders. In fact, twice a year I speak to groups of kids who are in the early stages of their high school careers. They are studying to become student aides to middle and elementary school kids in the coming semester. For these young, developing leaders, identifying triggers is critical, and I help them consider triggers within the framework of their own families. Here is what I cover with them.

Know Your Triggers
We all have buttons that get pushed from time to time—buttons that provoke anger, jealousy, pride, and more. Knowing what they are and who pushes them is vital information to have. As a great example, consider your siblings. Is there anyone better able to find your most sensitive nerve and pluck it than siblings? They seem to innately know what buttons to push to get an emotional response out of you.

So ask yourself this:

- What are your hot buttons?
- Who pushes them the most?
- Why does it make you react so emotionally?
- Which emotions do they provoke?

Knowing the *what, who, why,* and *which* will open the door to successfully managing these triggers.

Strategies
Recall the quote from military history introduced earlier to address this issue of strategy and the self-disciplined leader. Herman von Moltke, a German field marshal, said, "No plan of operations survives the first collision with the main body of the enemy."[1] In other words, while planning is important, leaders must always be prepared for unexpected change.

Emotionally Agile Leaders learn new strategies to deal with their emotions as life or career changes occur. Fortunately, a strategy that is developed today will always work in the future, right? Not exactly.

Here is where the need for agility is quite obvious. While plans and strategies are essential to being a successful leader, you must always keep in mind that plans can go out the window. Sometimes, you plan for A, B, or C, but the real situation you encounter is actually somewhere in the range of X, Y, or Z. Even if you had planned for D, E, F, or G, or most of the way down the alphabet, which is not practical on any level, you cannot reasonably strategize for every contingency. Therefore, you must be agile within the parameters of a self-disciplined life.

Coping Mechanisms

The Emotionally Agile Leader learns coping mechanisms and techniques to develop greater self-discipline. That is important because self-discipline is not a trait we are born with. It is a learned and developed habit.

In order to begin cultivating self-discipline coping mechanisms, you will need some awareness of the internal and external forces at work.

Know Your Why

Why do we need self-discipline? I think for most leaders, the quest for self-discipline is not completely altruistic. We desire the fruits of a self-disciplined life, although we don't actually desire the moment-by-moment attention to living a self-disciplined life. What we desire is to lead with discipline and effectiveness in a way that helps us achieve a disciplined approach to life and leadership. We just don't have a great love for the actual process of creating self-discipline.

In addition to the big *why*, there are some other questions that help Emotionally Agile Leaders cope with the challenges of being self-disciplined leaders. They cope by knowing the outcome they are seeking. Just what is your goal? Do you seek personal gain? Do you seek measurable results for the company? Having a clear understanding of where you want to go will help you strategize and cope in the present.

Emotionally Agile Leaders also cope by knowing what they are willing to sacrifice. Sacrifice and self-discipline go hand-in-hand, and sacrifice is every bit as rare. But if a leader has calculated the cost to the best of their ability, then they can cope with the unavoidable pain of self-discipline.

In addition, Emotionally Agile Leaders cope by knowing who they need to come alongside them in order to accomplish their goals. It has been said that no man is an island, and nowhere is that more true than in the area of leadership self-discipline. Self-discipline is not totally a solo endeavor. It has an accountability component, and that accountability must come from outside ourselves. We simply cannot hold ourselves accountable.

Emotionally Agile Leaders further cope by visualizing what success will look like when they achieve it. Self-discipline is a journey, not a destination. Therefore, there is a need to celebrate the little victories and milestones on the path to becoming a more self-disciplined leader.

Conflict

One key area that leaders must grow in is conflict. Can we all agree that some level of conflict is unavoidable? Can we also agree that how we face conflict and whether we resolve it say a great deal about our own leadership styles and abilities? Let's look at some of the core aspects of conflict.

Coping versus Resolving

The idea that conflict management is something to strive for has caused great harm in the leadership development community. I, for one, do not want to manage conflict. I want to resolve it.

Conflict is fundamentally a struggle between two parties. *Merriam-Webster* online defines it like this: "Competitive or opposing action of incompatibles: antagonistic state or action (as of divergent ideas, interests, or persons); mental struggle resulting from incompatible or opposing needs, drives, wishes, or external or internal demands."

Consider this statement by Warren Bennis, one of the foremost writers on leadership and organizational and management theory: "Leaders do not avoid, repress, or deny conflict, but rather see it as an opportunity."[2]

As an Emotionally Agile Leader, this is one of your primary responsibilities. You cannot delegate conflict resolution to one of your followers. Nor can you pretend that conflicts do not occur within the organization you lead.

Conflict Is Unavoidable

I have spent much of my adult life working in the corporate world during the week and serving in a nonprofit and volunteer organization on weeknights and weekends. Let me assure you, conflict is common to all organizations. Yes, you will even find conflict within churches and religious organizations. But we as leaders have the responsibility to sense conflict at its earliest stages and resolve it before it affects the entire organization.

Emotionally Agile Leaders do not avoid or run from conflict. I am not suggesting to seek out conflict or invent it where it does not exist. But great leaders must lead in times of calm and in times of conflict.

Conflict Ultimately Must Be Resolved

Resolution is an art as much as it is a science. The goal of conflict resolution is to assess and resolve disputes at the lowest level possible and to do so before disagreements escalate into something major.

Effective conflict resolution is accomplished by your ability as a leader to control two things: yourself (who you are) and your attitude (how you act or react). These are fundamental skills for Emotionally Agile Leaders. Human nature seeks to avoid conflict. So if conflict is not resolved and allowed to fester emotionally, it is human nature to separate ourselves from the conflict and isolate ourselves from its source. There is no leadership there, agile or otherwise.

The Cause of the Conflict
Lack of clarity, ambiguity, differing values, opposing objectives, different workplace cultures, and individual personality types set the stage for conflict. But the psychology behind conflict can be described as the fear of loss. A loss can have many forms. It can be the loss of stature, loss of financial interest, loss of influence, and many others. And when there is a conflict, people will fight in order to do the following:

- Stop the real loss or even just the sense of loss
- Lessen the impact of the loss
- Get back what they feel was lost

I already mentioned that it is beneficial to resolve conflict early and at the lowest level possible. In order to resolve conflict at its lowest level, it is necessary to identify our own interests and the interests of all those players in the conflict situation. Try to determine whether you are angry and why you are angry. Try to establish what will be necessary to resolve the conflict. These are the self-awareness and social-awareness components.

In other words:

- What is it that I really want?
- Why do I want it?
- What will happen if I don't get what I want?

As you answer these questions, you will begin to uncover the potential outcomes and identify the impact on yourself and your team based on those potential outcomes. Be honest. If you look at the situation objectively and try to see the conflict from its many facets, you will start to see how various solutions will potentially impact all parties. But you must be very open and self-aware.

What Does Good Conflict Resolution Look Like?
The characteristics of a good resolution may include some or all these characteristics:

- Any loss (real or imagined) or even a potential loss is addressed by the leader.
- A livable decision is reached for all parties involved. There is not always a win-win solution. Sometimes the best we will get is a livable solution.
- The resolution accounts for each party's interests and balances them against the overall interests of the organization.

Leaders, it is your job to operate in this environment in order to come to a successful resolution between the parties. Here is what you need to do:

- Know what you want.
- Pay close attention to any loss (real or perceived) when it is identified.
- Be flexible in finding a solution.
- Make a commitment that you are willing to live up to, whatever resolution is agreed on.

Some Closing Thoughts
Are you running from a conflict in your organization? If so, you're not showing good leadership. Or, on the flip side, are you itching for a fight? If so, you're also not showing good leadership.

You probably have several opportunities facing you right now. Remember, part of managing conflict assumes that conflict will always be around. Resolution deals with it and removes it from the day-to-day equation.

I'll leave you with a great anonymous quote I came across a while back. "Spending your days trying to avoid conflict is comparable to living in the ocean and trying to avoid getting wet. The task is impossible, and you just look silly."

Tools for Self-Discipline

Constantly Seeking Feedback
Seeking feedback may be one of the hardest methods of developing emotional agility. Our natural tendency is to avoid the kind of feedback we need most to develop our leadership potential. The key factor here is that we must constantly seek feedback. In fact, it should become ingrained in our communication process.

One of the most valuable tools for a leader is to have a realistic assessment of the situation. Consider this experience from my college days. I was a very active and involved undergrad. Live theater performance was a huge part of my life and had been since high school. Musical comedy was my favorite theatrical genre, and I was fortunate to have one of the leading roles in nearly every show I had been in. I can still remember most of my lines from *Anything Goes*, *Oklahoma*, and *Annie Get Your Gun*, just to name a few.

In college, I had a great relationship with my director. One night, after rehearsal and after we had reviewed all our lines from rehearsal, I was sitting on the edge of the stage while my director sat in the front row of the theater, as was her custom. I was feeling the need for some validation of my singing ability. Keep in mind that the key to musical comedy is comedic timing and the ability to vocally reach the back of the theater. So I asked her, "Rhonda, what do you really think of my singing ability?" She paused. She thought. And then she said something I have remembered for more than 37 years. She said, "Kevin, you are a great actor." And that was all she said.

She delivered a message about my singing ability that helped me have some perspective and manage my expectations. In that moment, I was able to realize what was realistic and what was unrealistic in terms of my vocal and singing abilities. And she delivered the message in a way that did not devastate me. I went on to spend more time on stage. But I also spent some time in the wings and began doing some directing. Her emotional agility to answer a tough question from a fairly high-strung actor was just what I needed.

Feedback like that comes through a deep and trust-filled relationship. But we still need feedback, even when we don't have that level of trust built over a long period of time. The simplest and most effective way to get feedback is to ask for it. But we need to ask for it in a constructive manner and not out of a sense of need for positive reinforcement and encouragement. We must make sure that the one giving the feedback can do so without fear of anger or defensiveness on our part. We need to make sure they know we genuinely are seeking their feedback, their observations, and their perceptions.

Post-Mortems after Key Events

Okay, the title of this section is a little morbid. But stick with me for a minute or two. I have used this method many times with clients in a consulting scenario. The approach takes a look at what exactly happens during an event so all stakeholders can understand the event clearly. Not all will see it the same way. But with enough individual views, a collective view will emerge.

This method can be particularly helpful when there is already an acknowledgment that there are some issues that need to be addressed. The approach requires a high degree of trust because it naturally focuses on the negatives of what took place. It is very similar to the critiques I received in theater at the end of a performance or rehearsal. The best critiques will include all the following components:

- *The Good.* The review team needs to list the things that went well during the meeting or event. What worked well? What flowed naturally from beginning to end? What examples of positive feedback did you note during the event?
- *The Bad.* The review team needs to also list what flopped. Be honest. Not everything was stellar. In other words, let's acknowledge the so-called elephant in the room. Remember to clearly articulate the problem with what happened and avoid attacking people, performers, or personnel.
- *The Missing.* The review team needs to list what was lacking in the event. In other words, what could you have done that would have made it a better experience for the audience or the organization? In my experience, this is the least used category but can often provide some stunning insights into where our focus should be in the future.
- *The Confusing.* The review team needs to list what didn't make sense to the audience or the organization. Don't assume that everyone understood the message of the event the way you intended it. Just because you said it a certain way doesn't mean everyone heard it that way.

Now that we have our list, what do we do with it?

Here is where Emotionally Agile Leaders stand out. They will review the items on the list and develop strategies to maximize the good, minimize the bad, fill in the missing, and clarify the confusing. Emotionally Agile Leaders will draw from those around them who have specific skills that can address each of the four items of the post-mortem review.

When was the last time you did a post-mortem of an event or a significant meeting in your organization? Many times, we don't take a hard look at our activities for fear of what it may reveal. Be fearless today. Take a good, hard look and see what you find. You will be better for doing so.

What Does the Emotionally Agile Leader Do?

Become the kind of leader that people would follow voluntarily, even if you had no title or position.
—Brian Tracy

Let's wrap up the key points of this section.

Emotionally Agile Leaders use the awareness of their triggers to avoid or minimize a trigger event. They identify them and take specific steps to provide the necessary emotional distance to respond in a way that is disciplined, helpful, and not harmful in any given situation.

Emotionally Agile Leaders develop a well-disciplined strategy to take immediate corrective action if an emotional outbreak occurs. They have a contingency plan in place.

Emotionally Agile Leaders employ various coping mechanisms to increase their self-discipline and self-control.

Emotionally Agile Leaders understand and act to resolve conflict and not just merely find a way to cope with it. They are able to bring parties together in an emotionally acceptable way and ferret out the root of the conflict. They help the parties see the conflict from alternate perspectives in a way that brings about a resolution and ends the conflict.

OBSERVANT

Emotionally Agile Leaders Are Aware of Their Social Interactions

The day the soldiers stop bringing you their problems is the day you stopped leading them. They have either lost confidence that you can help them or concluded that you do not care. Either case is a failure of leadership.

—Colin Powell

We've spent the first part of this book discussing how leaders can better understand and discipline themselves. Now it's time to turn our attention outward. As important as acting on self-awareness through self-discipline is to leaders, awareness of ourselves is of little value if there is no emotional awareness of those around us. Now that we better understand ourselves, we can logically turn our attention to understanding other people.

What Should the Emotionally Agile Leader Learn?

Emotionally Agile Leaders are observant. They have a heightened sense of awareness of the folks they come in contact with in their various social settings throughout the day. They can identify the emotional states of those they interact with on a regular basis. They are also aware that followers can often be a reflection of the attitudes of leaders. Let's start this section by seeing how we can better understand people.

Projecting

I recently wrote an article about a certain amount of reflecting that comes back to us based on what we are projecting. It is true that our followers will reflect whatever we project to them from a leadership style perspective. It is just that simple. It is also just that scary.

Many years ago when my children were very young, I was commenting about their behavior (and by behavior, I mean misbehavior) in Sunday school one morning. I jokingly said they must have learned that behavior while playing with other children. The teacher's response was humorous, but it stung my heart. It became one of the most haunting little statements that anyone has ever made to me when I was a young parent. He said, "Children only do what they see at home."

I was mortified. What if that was true? (And I believe that it is to a large extent.) What if those little eyes really are watching my every move? Fast forward many years later, and I can tell you that my children have grown into incredible adults. They are wonderful parents and role models for their own children.

But stay with me, please. This is not about parenting. It is really about leadership and understanding that our followers are a reflection of what they perceive in us. In other words, how do they perceive the leadership message or methodology we project? And can we observe what we are projecting by how followers reflect our leadership?

Knowing a positive leadership style and then projecting it will have a lot to do with whether or not you are successful as a leader. We must also objectively observe how our followers perceive and reflect our leadership back to us and ultimately forward to their own followers. Here are a few things that leaders who are emotionally intelligent and emotionally agile will project:

- Because they are self-aware, they have the ability to respond and adapt their leadership methods when the reflection they are seeing is not what they intend to project.
- Because they are both self-aware and socially aware, they have a presence about them that is polished, professional, and poised, even under pressure.
- Because they are self-disciplined, they project authority and confidence without being bossy and braggadocious.

Reflecting

Equally important, here are some things that will be reflected back to us if we are projecting positive leadership styles and messages:

- Our followers will reflect peace as a result of our ability to respond and adapt to the emotional leadership landscape.
- Our followers will reflect confidence in us, in the organization, and in themselves when we are poised and professional in tense moments.
- Our followers will reflect pride that is rooted and grounded in real accomplishments and not just hollow words.

Let's face it, you can't control how someone perceives you. Their perceptions will always be viewed through the lens of their own emotions and experiences. You can do everything right and still not be perceived in a positive manner. But we can and we must make every effort to project a positive leadership style and have that projection validated objectively through peer reviews and 360-degree feedback from our followers.

If our followers really are a reflection of our leadership, then how do your followers look to you as you observe them?

Observing Is Just the Start

I cannot separate observation from action. An Emotionally Agile Leader will not simply make an observation without applying that observation to the situation. One of the key messages of this book is that I want to help train your observations and your skills until they become second nature to you. In other words, I want to get leaders to a point where there is little gap between observations and actions. Taking action about things you observe should in some ways become an instinctual process. And if not instinctual, it at least becomes so rapidly processed in our brains that to the untrained eye, it appears to be a reflexive or instinctive response.

Managing Social Interactions with Agility

It is so important that we develop the ability to spot potential individuals who may create a negative outcome in organizations. But we must go beyond mere observation and awareness, as important as they are. The Emotionally Agile Leader must then respond to them in a way that will create a positive outcome for the person and the organization.

As your observation skills develop, so will your ability to respond with emotional agility. Consider these common social creatures who can be found in any organization and some means and methods to manage them and their character traits.

The Yes Person

Wouldn't you love to be surrounded by people who agree with everything you say? Wouldn't it be great if your closest advisors thought every idea you had was a great one? Well, the truth of the matter is that being surrounded by folks who will never challenge you and your decisions is bad for you and bad for the organization you lead.

It's natural to want to be surrounded by people who support and praise you all the time. Having people who are always in your corner, no matter the issue or circumstance, is comforting. But these people are not necessarily yes people.

Yes people tend to be unwilling to think creatively or take initiative. They wait for the leader to announce an idea or position and then immediately jump on the bandwagon with a full-throttled affirmation that the idea is the greatest. The danger of being surrounded with these types of individuals is that we will slowly but surely believe we always make great decisions. These individuals will shut down any further creative solutions and ideas once the leader has indicated a position. When they influence the social interactions between you and your followers, they inhibit the growth and success of the team.

The Emotionally Agile Leader loves people who love and appreciate them. However, leaders also know that team members bring added value when their input is tempered with objectivity and originality. Yes people can become objective people as the Emotionally Agile Leader works with them and helps them increase their own self-awareness.

The Negative Person

Saturday Night Live popularized the negative person when they created the Debbie Downer character. We all know someone like that. No matter how exceptional the idea or who comes up with it, the negative person will find fault with it and prophesy its imminent demise if we are foolish enough to try to accomplish it.

The biggest problem with negativity is that it is contagious and can affect the entire organization if left unchecked. But negativity is not always overt. It tends to be covert in nature. The person who is usually negative is often not negative to your face or in an open way. They will most often gather one or two around them after the meeting is over and begin to express why the idea is just not going to work. If one or two are willing to listen to this Debbie Downer, they also tend to be predisposed to a bit of negative emotional thinking. They will typically share that negativity with other people in the organization.

Emotionally Agile Leaders are always on the lookout for little enclaves of negativity. Once negativity is identified, these leaders will deal with the negative emotional feelings in a way that turns them around or helps them find a role within the organization that will minimize their influence. Straightforward, direct communication is best with these individuals. They must become aware that you are observing the negativity and the impact it is having on the organization. And unless their negativity is a pathological problem, consider giving them a visible and obvious task for which they are accountable. If they get rid of the negative image emanating from them, they may look for a way to produce a positive outcome for themselves and thus for you and the team.

The Influencer
The influencer is someone the Emotionally Agile Leader must identify very early in their leadership tenure in an organization.

Identifying influencers was something I struggled with very early in my leadership career. One story comes to mind as I write this section.

The story begins with an idea. The idea was that in order to increase the effectiveness and reach of the organization that we (the influencer and I) both loved and served, a change was necessary to how we served the people of that organization. It was my idea that if we radically altered how we delivered the message to the members, we would see greater attendance, greater involvement, and greater engagement. At least that was the idea.

However, the influencer and I found ourselves with opposite opinions about what that significant change should be. We were both fully invested in the organization and wanted it to succeed. We were dear friends and both had the best interests of the organization in mind. We both knew some kind of change was necessary to stop the steady decline in attendance and participation. We just differed on what that change should look like.

I felt it was necessary to make a bold, radical change. I felt that that change alone would cause such a burst of energy and enthusiasm that we would be resoundingly successful. So we employed a full-speed-ahead process. We charged forward and were absolutely convinced we would be successful.

But here was the problem. I overlooked the influencer and underestimated his influence in the organization. I didn't see the level of leadership he possessed. Therefore, I never took the time to sell the idea to him and the need for change. I just assumed that if the idea was good and I pushed hard enough, I would be successful.

Here is the lesson I learned 25 years ago. I learned the importance of bringing *all* the stakeholders together and including them in the change management process. Actually, I learned the importance of bringing them into the idea generation process that precedes the change. It is not about who is right or who has the better idea. It is about inclusion and selling the idea *before* you make the change. You cannot sell the idea after you make a radical change.

That incident taught me that leadership is not about position and authority. It is about influence. I had the position and the authority, but someone else had the influence. I should have realized that at the time, and perhaps the outcome of the change would have been different. I know for sure that had I been a more Emotionally Agile Leader, I would have recognized it before it became a problem.

In complete transparency, I recognize that the idea was good, but the execution was not. So the change we attempted did not bring about the results we had hoped for. Was it because of my failure to recognize the role of the influencer? We may never know since we cannot go back in time and try a different approach. But I do know that it didn't work the way I executed it, and it taught me something valuable. It was not a total loss since it provided insights I would not have otherwise experienced.

The Emotionally Agile Leader brings the influencer into the decision-making process and leverages their leadership to maximize the organization's success.

The Toxic One

Give this idea of the toxic person a very wide berth. Steer clear as much as you can. The Emotionally Agile Leader probably already knows who this person is—every organization has one. They are just not good to be around. They go beyond mere negativity and are more like poison. That is a harsh comparison, but they can even be like cancer to an organization.

Wow! That sounds harsh (and it is). The toxic one causes damage to everything they touch. What is it about them that makes them toxic? In my opinion, the thing that makes them toxic is that they are drawn to whatever is harmful or hurtful in any given situation. They have the capacity to magnify that hurt and then project it or carry it to other parts of the organization. They are, in essence, bent on destruction.

Sometimes, these types of individuals cannot be moderated and must be removed from the organization. The Emotionally Agile Leader is more about quick responses than about long, drawn-out psychological care for the toxic ones. And sometimes, just like in a physical body, a cancer must be cut out in order to save the rest of the body.

The Emotionally Agile Leader is not without hope in this situation and must deal with this one as directly as they deal with the negative person, if not more so. Indeed, the leader must deal with the toxic person with all due haste before the toxicity spreads and infects the entire team or organization. Here is where the swiftness of agility is important so the team does not suffer the infectious nature of this individual.

The Passive-Aggressive One
The passive-aggressive person may be a little harder to identify, but one of the most defining characteristics in this type of person is the significant disconnect between what the person says and what the person does. Their communication tends to be indirect and obtuse. It is indirect since they avoid any face-to-face contact where there is the possibility of conflict. It is obtuse since you cannot take their statements at face value. It is hard for even an Emotionally Agile Leader to interact

with the passive-aggressive one because you are never quite sure what you are dealing with.

Passive-aggressive behavior is often expressed through procrastination. Rather than tell you they have no intention of doing what is being asked of them, they put it off and then put it off again until there is no way it can be done. Then, they never accept the blame for the lack of progress or success. Related to this behavior is the tendency to intentionally underperform when given a task to complete—after all, if they perform poorly, perhaps they will not be asked to do it again.

At first glance, passive-aggressive people may seem pleasant and warm. They can appear to be kind and complimentary. It is only after you step away from the interaction that you realize that the compliment was actually masquerading as a cheap shot. Not only will they take a cheap shot, but they like to take the last shot. Even when a conflict has been reconciled, they slip in one last insult that can easily reverse the resolution.

The Emotionally Agile Leader should take a direct approach with this individual. When their communication is obtuse, the Emotionally Agile Leader goes back to them and asks for a direct response, confirming that what was heard is what the person really intended to communicate. And the leader helps the passive-aggressive one come to a mutually agreed schedule that will help provide the milestones in increments of time so they do not get too far behind. This is a little more work for the leader, but Emotionally Agile Leaders see themselves as not only demonstrating good habits but also helping employees form new habits that will help them escape the passive-aggressive trap.

The Social Butterfly

Not every character you observe on your team will have the same level of impact. In other words, when you are observing your team and determining where the problems are coming from, the social butterflies on your team might not jump to the forefront of your mind. After all, their outgoing, friendly nature livens up the team. However, they can cause some problems for the Emotionally Agile Leader.

For instance, they can distract the rest of the team. Their need for conversation pulls people away from their work. They're so friendly that they have the ability to suck people into their coffee-room conversations. And before you know it, they have eaten up an hour of someone's time and distracted others around them.

They also inhibit progress and delay schedules. Their contagious chatter and sense of humor (and the need to share that with everyone on the team) can lead to missed deadlines and unfinished work for all. The loss of time is multiplied with every person engaged with a social butterfly.

And finally, social butterflies can be gossipers. Many of them know all the good stuff and are willing to share it with anyone who is willing to listen. And if they don't have any good gossip, they will make something up in order to have a reason to share with those who will listen.

The Emotionally Agile Leader finds a way to help the social butterfly channel their naturally social nature into actions that will benefit the organization. These individuals can make great communications directors for a project team. Give them a message you need to disseminate, and they will do it. But be sure to provide the message, and do not leave it up to that person at first. Giving them authorship before they demonstrate competency means they could slip into bad habits of making stuff up if they don't have a script or message.

The Oblivious One

Being smart doesn't mean you are perceptive. There is a Japanese phrase, *kuuki yomenai*, which literally translates into English as "can't read the air." I love that translation (sometimes the English language is not as descriptive as other languages).

This inability to read the air can be used to describe someone who doesn't pick up on social cues or is unaware of other people's moods or emotional expressions. Clearly, the oblivious one would rate low on both the self-awareness and social-awareness scales. Therefore, the leader must be aware and compensate for their obliviousness.

The Emotionally Agile Leader compensates by providing feedback early and often to the oblivious one. Since they can't read the signs, an Emotionally Agile Leader will need to be direct and proactive with them. By now, you have probably noticed that directness is a critical skill for the Emotionally Agile Leader.

The Time Sucker

There are certainly aspects of the time sucker built into some of the other characters that Emotionally Agile Leaders need to observe. The time sucker is a very needy individual. They will spend as much time in your office as you will allow. They are often asking questions and seeking your advice. Having one of your team members come to you for guidance can feel good, but at some point, you look at your watch, and an hour and a half has gone by without an end to the little impromptu one-on-one session.

This character really wants to do well for you and the organization—they just lack the confidence or initiative to leave your side and figure some things out for themselves. They find comfort in knowing you will always be there for them. The problem comes when they monopolize your time to the detriment of your own work, preventing you from spending any time developing and mentoring others on the team. The Emotionally Agile Leader must recognize this person and how they negatively impact the organization in subtle ways.

The Emotionally Agile Leader needs to give time suckers tasks. They need lots of tasks, and the tasks need to be succinct and well-defined. Time suckers also need predefined times you will be available to them. The Emotionally Agile Leader cannot practice an open-door policy with everyone in the organization.

The Deceiver
The deceiver must be identified and weeded out with all due haste. Not only is their dishonesty problematic to your direct relationship with them, it also reflects negatively on the entire organization. You must first assess how the deceiver impacts you as the leader. Once you have assessed that, you must determine their impact on the entire organization. Sometimes the damage is minor, only causing you to become distrustful of the deceptive person, but other times, there is a real negative impact on the organization. That damage can be the company's reputation or even financial loss.

I once had a sales manager and sales team who called on me and my team. The problem was that he could not be trusted. He was patently dishonest, and his dishonesty was the easiest to spot of anyone I had ever known. Anytime he attempted to be deceitful, he would reach up and stroke his eyebrow, twisting it in his fingers nervously. When he returned to the truth, he relaxed his hands and held them in front of his body. It didn't take long to be able to tell what he was saying in terms of truthfulness just by watching his hands. But not everyone is that obvious.

The Emotionally Agile Leader must be keenly observant and constantly looking for the clues that everyone will provide if you look closely enough. There is not nearly as much doing as there is observing when it comes to this individual. But the doing is more about identifying and then minimizing their impact on the reputation of the team. The easy solution may be to get rid of such a person. The greater leadership challenge may be working with them and resolving their character issues that have caused them to eschew integrity and truth.

The Traitor

Emotionally Agile Leaders must also be able to spot the traitor. Why did Dante make the traitor's betrayal (treachery) the worst sin—surpassing even rape, theft, and murder? I don't know. But treachery is one of the most damaging things to a leader and to an organization. That damage goes deep, creating an emotional hurt often hard to overcome.

These characters are the stuff of history and great literature. Just reflect for a moment on Benedict Arnold, Iago from Shakespeare's *Othello*, Edmund in *The Chronicles of Narnia*, or Fredo Corleone in *The Godfather Part II*. The reality is that you cannot have the betrayal without first having the presence of trust (and even so-called love). It is not betrayal and you are not a traitor unless you are first trusted by the leader and the organization.

This book is not a treatise on the importance of forgiveness and restoration. Rather, it is a practical guide to becoming an Emotionally Agile Leader who must identify the traitor, isolate them, and minimize their assault on the emotional health of the organization.

The Emotionally Agile Leader finds the response to the traitor to be much the same as the deceiver. Therefore, it is also about isolating the traitor from further impact. The Emotionally Agile Leader uses emotional maturity to disassociate the betrayal from the betrayer. Perhaps this is one of the hardest things for the Emotionally Agile Leader to do. And, like working with the deceiver, the additional challenge exists when it is in the best interest of all to retain the individual and seek reparation to the damage caused by the treachery.

What Does the Emotionally Agile Leader Do?

Emotional Agile Leaders use their self-awareness and social observations to assess individuals and situations. That observation and assessment informs them of the potential pitfalls they may encounter.

But more importantly, they use these observations to formulate a positive approach to the individual and the social setting in a swift, confident manner. They have developed the skills to manage their own emotions, and they have developed tactics and methodologies to create positive outcomes from challenging social interactions. They accomplish this swiftly, if not instinctively, as they observe, assess, and respond to leadership challenges.

INFLUENTIAL

Emotionally Agile Leaders Manage
Their Social Interactions

*The greatest ability in business is to get along
with others and to influence their actions.*
—John Hancock

One of the difficulties of the modern organizational management theory today is the lack of clear lines of authority. Many times, leaders are thrust into situations without the ability to directly control anything. Instead, they must fall back on one of the basic identifiers of leadership: influence.

Emotionally Agile Leaders are influencers. They recognize that they may not always have direct authority or control over a social interaction or a group of individuals. However, they realize that leadership is not about power but about the proper use of influence to create mutually beneficial outcomes for the project, organization, team, and each individual on the team.

What Should the Emotionally Agile Leader Learn?

Leaders should learn ways to turn emotional situations around and create positive outcomes when other people can't find a way. They should also learn ways to leverage the EI of others. This is not manipulation—it is simply leveraging what leaders know about themselves and about those around them to get the best out of the team.

Leaders should also use their influence for the good of the organization, even if it is not for their own benefit. This is not a natural response for many—self-preservation and acting in our own best interest is natural. Notice that I did not say self-preservation is always a bad thing. We must consider ourselves and any situation that may impact our lives in the long term.

Finally, leaders create a sort of bank account of influence to draw from when the situation warrants it. Leaders must understand that basic human nature shows that as leaders, we should create a well of good will from which to draw when needed. Emotionally Agile Leaders who have acted consistently with care and concern will be given the necessary leeway when a social interaction warrants an unpopular response.

Key Methods

There are some key methods to employ as we develop our emotional agility.

Slow Down to Get to Know Your Followers

One of the factors most important for me in my days as a professional speaker was a maxim I learned from the former actor who taught me all I needed to know about professional public speaking. He taught me that I needed to know my audience before I spoke to them. Those were wise words.

Leaders, how well do you know your followers? Just what do you know about them? Do you even know them at all? These are tough questions, but they are questions we must consider. Knowing the answers will provide us with the insights we need into the lives and personalities of our team members.

Let's assume for a moment that you accept the value of knowing your followers. How can you get to know them better? Consider the following ideas:

- *Go to them.* Visit them. If you regularly have one-on-ones with your followers, consider having the next one at their office or sitting at their desk. Why? You will see the things that are important to them by what they have displayed on their desks. Is it a picture of their family? Is it their motorcycle? Is their favorite sports team obvious? You may not ever know some of these pieces that make up the whole person unless you make the effort to go to their space.
- *Go with them.* Go with them the next time they need to make a presentation. This does not simply apply to sales organizations. Your followers may be making other kinds of presentations, and your presence in the audience can demonstrate that you have great confidence in them. You will also get a chance to see them and share some feedback based on your personal observations.
- *Go for them.* Go for them and represent them sometime at an event where they would ordinarily go. Once you get there, take the opportunity to mingle with the folks your follower would usually be mingling with. Ask them for their thoughts and insights about your follower. You will get a chance to see your follower from a whole new perspective.
- *Now I know. What now?* I made an assumption earlier that you accept the value of knowing your followers. My final assumption is that you will take the knowledge you have gained and use it to build your followers in such a way that they can become leaders themselves. Just as professional speakers know their audiences, knowing

your followers will provide the insights into their personalities and emotional makeup that you will need in order to communicate with them effectively at the highest level. You will truly know them. And that's a powerful thing.

Communicate Trustworthiness

Culture says that the end result is all that matters. That is false. How we achieve results is also important. Emotionally Agile Leaders develop good work habits early in their careers. Character matters. When times of adversity come to your organization, people will follow the leader they trust the most, even when they don't know where the leader is taking them.

How long this process of building and communicating trustworthiness takes will vary. It will take time to build trust and confidence with the ones who follow you. Even those predisposed to follow you, or who are part of a direct line of authority under you, will take some time to trust you.

Exhibit Confidence

Emotionally Agile Leaders need confidence that the difficult decisions they must make are the right decisions for the team and the overall organization. And they must lead with confidence so they can assuage the doubts and fears of their team. Perhaps one of the most confident messages ever delivered was by Julius Caesar. In 47 BC, he was asked for a report on his recent military exploits. The Roman Senate wanted to know what happened on the eastern edge of the Empire. Julius Caesar replied, *"Veni, vidi, vici"*—"I came, I saw, I conquered."

That is about as confidently succinct as it can be. In it, there is a statement about logistics—I came. There is a statement about planning—I saw. And there is a statement about the execution of the plan—I conquered.

What are the emotionally agile leadership implications of communicating like Caesar? I think confident leaders have a brevity of speech that still communicates powerfully and effectively. That confidence allows them to shortcut much of the chatter and nonsense of communication. Leaders at the highest levels do not have the luxury of small talk with the people they deal with. So they adapt their style and take a minimalist approach. This communication style exhibits and exudes confidence.

Inspire Confidence
It is not enough to exhibit confidence on our own. We must inspire it in those around us. Emotionally Agile Leaders need to manifest and demonstrate courage and determination at all times. When the team gets discouraged, they need to be able to look up, see you, and draw confidence from your demeanor. The team needs to feel that although things are falling apart around them, you are still in control, and you will lead them out of this mess.

Calmness and composure are as contagious as panic. Leaders who project their own calmness to those around them see that calmness reflected back as their followers draw confidence and courage from them.

Perhaps one of the greatest examples in recent years of bringing calm to a crisis situation is the emergency landing of a US Airways commuter plane in the Hudson River. Moments after takeoff, Flight 1549 struck a flock of geese, causing its engines to fail. Captain Chesley Sullenberger made one of the most remarkable emergency landings in aviation history by piloting the plane between buildings on both shores and bringing it down safely in the middle of the Hudson River, saving the lives of all 155 onboard.

Sullenberger said this in an interview with *Parade* magazine:

> It wasn't until about 90 seconds before we hit the water that I spoke to the passengers. I wanted to be very direct. I didn't want to sound agitated or alarmed. I wanted to sound professional. "This is the captain. Brace for impact![1]

Imagine what must have been going through his mind. He had the lives of 155 people in his well-trained hands. He knew every second mattered. Yet he took the necessary seconds to make sure his emotions were under control and his voice calm. At a time when every thought needed to be focused on a precise sequence of emergency landing procedures, he knew that the choice of his words and even the tone of his voice would send a powerful message to the passengers. Captain Sullenberger understood what great leaders know—their emotions are contagious. And great leaders bring confidence and calm to the situation.

Listen to Understand and Not to Speak

We often assume that leaders can verbalize, but can they listen? Listening is often a hard skill for leaders. They are accustomed to speaking, taking charge, and giving strategic direction.

How many times have we heard of people in significant leadership roles who have trouble communicating at home? Have you ever been told by someone in your family that they are not your employee? Ouch! It hurts when we hear that. Unfortunately, in both the workplace and at home, we find ourselves listening just enough to provide an answer but not enough to demonstrate we truly care about what the person is saying. And all too often, when we interrupt and provide an answer, it is the wrong answer.

Being overly chatty or verbose is not optimal. Being silent or overly non-verbal is also not optimal. Like Captain Sullenberger, a measured communication style can bolster our leadership impact.

PROLIFERATIVE

Emotionally Agile Leaders
Create More Leaders

*If you want to build a ship, don't drum up the men to
gather wood, divide the work, and give orders. Instead,
teach them to yearn for the vast and endless sea.*

—Antoine de Saint-Exupéry[1]

One of the truths I hold most dear to my heart is that one of my primary functions as a leader is to build more leaders—not more followers. Followers are an almost inevitable result of good leadership. But followers are not the goal. They are a by-product. The hallmark of great leaders is that they are proliferative, reproducing more leaders to join them in the great challenge and journey of leadership.

Thanksgiving has been known for many traditions. One of them is a football game. The Dallas Cowboys have played on Thanksgiving Day every year since 1966, and that, my friend, is a tradition.

I became a Steelers fan in my teen years. They were awesome in the 1970s, and the Cowboys weren't bad either. But the best thing to be said about the Cowboys back then was their coach—Tom Landry.

There have been some amazing coaches in professional football—John Madden, Vince Lombardi, Mike Ditka, and

Tony Dungy. They are only a few of the great coaches who have walked the chalk on the sidelines. But beyond their ability to instruct and motivate with Xs and Os, consider for a moment one of the key tasks of a football coach as the leader of a team. He must get his guys to do what is tough and tiring in order to achieve what they all really want—to win the Super Bowl.

And he must get some of them to step up and lead the team on the field where the coach cannot go. John Madden had Kenny Stabler. Vince Lombardi had Bart Starr. Mike Ditka had Jim McMahon. And Tony Dungy had Peyton Manning. Some of the quarterbacks on that short list were not great leaders off the field. But on any given Sunday, they could carry a team on their shoulders.

Ralph Nader once said, "The function of leadership is to produce more leaders, not more followers."[2] Inadequate leaders just create followers. But truly great leaders, Emotionally Agile Leaders, produce more leaders.

But creating leaders is easier said than done. Consider for a moment some wisdom from past generations, which may require some translation for our modern culture: "You can lead a horse to water, but you can't make him drink."

How many times have you heard that statement? It's an old bit of country wisdom. The problem is this. You can bring your horse to the water trough, but if he ain't thirsty, then he ain't drinkin'.

Now, consider an update to that piece of rural wisdom. "You can lead a horse to water, but you can't make him drink. However, you can salt his oats."

In days gone by, our forefathers knew that if a horse was sick, weak, or in danger of going down, you could put a little salt in its oats, which might encourage the horse to drink to satisfy its thirst. It's a great analogy of one of the skills we need as leaders from time to time.

We will have reluctant followers. Their reluctance may be the result of factors beyond our control. Nevertheless, we have to lead them, even when they are not exactly in the mood to be led. And we must make them yearn for leadership.

What is the Emotionally Agile Leader's lesson here? I think it is that as leaders, it is our job to create a thirst for the things that will help the organization (and these reluctant followers) grow and be successful in the mission for which they have been chosen. One of my favorite leadership quotes paints a picture of this much better than I can and headlines this chapter of the book. Consider these words attributed to Antoine de Saint-Exupéry, a French aristocrat, writer, poet, and pioneering aviator both before and during the Second World War: "If you want to build a ship, don't drum up the men to gather wood, divide the work, and give orders. Instead, teach them to yearn for the vast and endless sea." Isn't that just a more refined way of saying that you need to salt their oats from time to time?

I think it is all too easy to drum up people and start ordering them about. But that doesn't sound like leadership—it sounds like a dictatorship. And did you get the methodology that comes from this quote? It indicates that one of our roles as leaders is to be teachers. We are to teach and inspire those around us to yearn for something bigger than the tasks at hand.

Many leaders struggle with the internal conflict of being task-driven or mission-driven on the one hand and being visionary, inspirational, and educational on the other hand.

What kind of leader are you? Are you creating a thirst and a yearning? If you are, you will be creating more leaders and not just more followers.

The point I want to focus on for the remainder of this book is the need to be proliferative and duplicate our leadership in those around us. The Emotionally Agile Leader realizes that the real goal of a great leader is not to create more followers but to create more leaders. Leadership is getting someone to do what they don't want to do to achieve what they want to achieve.

Managers versus Leaders

Much has been written about the stark differences between managers and leaders, so I will not belabor the point. I will only say that the quote attributed to Antoine de Saint-Exupéry points out the differences in perspective and approach when it comes to managers and leaders.

I am fairly certain that ships could not be built without solid management skills. Someone must gather wood and give orders. Those are the managers. But I want someone to lead me who inspires me to yearn for the vast and endless sea. More importantly, I want to be that kind of leader to others.

The problem is that the two terms—*managers* and *leaders*—have been viewed as synonymous. Those who would be leaders have fled from leadership because they don't want to be managers or to even be viewed as managers. It seems today that no one wants to be a manager. I know I certainly no longer have that desire.

At one point in my career, I had more than 90 people who reported directly or indirectly to me. Those were some of the most unfulfilling years of my career. And rather than focus on the 90, I chose to focus on one or two and do my best to influence them, mentor them, and help them grow and develop leadership skills of their own. Those were the activities that made management bearable for me.

Making a Difference

Everyone needs an acronym every now and then to help remember things or get a better grasp of concepts. So I will give you an acronym, LEAD, to help you better understand how to be an Emotionally Agile Leader, so you can make a difference in your home, at your job, where you volunteer, and in your community.

L – Learn. Each of us must invest in ourselves in order to learn how to become a better leader. Although many folks are naturally gifted with leadership traits and tendencies, many are not. So, it is imperative that we each develop ways to learn from other recognized leaders in our contemporary culture and cultivate a good historical knowledge of leaders from our past. For example, read about leaders such as Jack Welch and George Patton. Don't get distracted by some of their personal or family foibles, but focus on the public leadership they displayed.

As we have seen, leaders must learn to recognize leadership potential in those around them. It is a learned behavior, and our natural tendency is to only recognize those things that bring us personal, tangible benefits. There is a part of every leader that loves to quantify their leadership. How many friends or followers do you have on Facebook or LinkedIn? I bet you know.

E – Earn. Each of us must earn the right to lead. We must lead in the little things before we can expect to be given great leadership responsibility. You don't often make it from the mail room to the board room in a week. But you will earn the right to lead through time and through trial and error. Unfortunately, many in the younger generation have never experienced trial and error. They have grown up in a culture where everyone is a winner and is given a ribbon for just participating. Leadership is earned.

A – Admire. Each of us must find another leader whom we admire for their leadership abilities. And this time, unlike the first item of the acronym, character counts. In fact, character is everything in this regard. Here is where you will learn the personal traits that make the leader great. Here is where you will find the leaders making the most lasting impacts. These people will most likely not be the captains of industry. Rather, they will be the head deacon in a church or the director of a local, compassionate ministry that is really making a difference and drawing volunteers to reach people in their greatest need. These leaders will seldom be seen on the 6:00 news or on the front page of a glossy magazine. But they will be men and women whom you would like to use as a model for your life and leadership style.

D – Duplicate. Each of us must find someone to pour ourselves into and then mentor them to become a great leader. Leadership is not about creating followers. It is about creating other leaders. Personally, I am deeply committed to this even though it is a time-consuming process.

So what is the point of this simple acronym? It is to drive home the points above and ask the following questions:

- Who are you learning from these days?
- What are you doing to earn the right to lead?
- Whom do you admire and want to pattern your leadership style after?
- Whom are you investing in so you can duplicate and reproduce more leaders for today and tomorrow?

Whom Should I Influence?

We live in a corporate culture that seeks the graduate with the 4.0 GPA. I see this every day in my corporate job. My current company goes after the best of the best from the top engineering schools in the country. I am not saying that this approach is wrong. After all, it is pretty hard to argue when you look at the economic success we have had over the last 147 years. But the issue is not whom the corporation should look for but rather whom I should look for.

How to Select a Protégé or Mentee

Give me a B student who worked two part-time jobs while going to school. That person will have already learned some important lessons about managing competing priorities. That person has already learned how to move in two very different worlds—the academic world and the real world. We all know the academic world is nothing like the real world.

They almost certainly will have developed communication skills and powers of persuasion from those times when they had to pull an extra shift at the restaurant and didn't get their paper turned in on time and yet were able to persuade the professor to accept it with little or no penalty to their grade.

They also tend to already have underlying emotional intelligence and the ability to be agile. This causes them to be generally well liked by their peers. They are not the life of the party because they are working two jobs, remember? But people enjoy being around them and tend to drift toward them rather than away from them.

That is the kind of person I am always looking for. They actually make up a huge segment of the population—they are not the bell of the curve. They are on the upward slope and are often hungry for opportunity, anxious to show the world they are a better, more well-rounded people than the 4.0 students.

But there are also signs that point to whom you should avoid. Avoid those who already seem to believe they know it all. Avoid those who are looking to you for self-serving means. Sometimes, a protégé's true motivation is not easy to identify, so I must constantly be diligent in that area. Because of my current position of influence, I have many who seek my advice and mentorship. However, an initial call or meeting over coffee with them quickly reveals that they are really just looking for a back-door entrance into a major corporation where they hope to build their personal network for economic gain. Sadly, I have to shut these people down as quickly as I become aware of their underlying motivation.

How Can I Influence Future Leaders?

Okay, I have my leadership protégé. Now what? What do I do with them?

Be Sure Your Influence Is Welcome

Having provided the warning above that some may seek your influence for personal gain, it remains that the mark of an Emotionally Agile Leader is that their influence is welcomed by those they lead. In fact, their influence is sought after and desired by some of their followers who yearn to be leaders. As leaders, we must foster relationships that create value for our followers in exchange for the time they are within our circle of influence.

That value can be monetary, of course. In other words, your positive influence and mentorship will make them more valuable to their organization. And that value is most often expressed monetarily through their overall compensation package. Leaders are not coin-operated, and truly great leaders lead for selfless reasons. But we cannot overlook the fact that in a culture desperate for leadership, many organizations will reward their leaders in a tangible way.

Look around you. Is there someone whose influence you would like in your life or on your leadership journey? Then go speak to them. Tell them you have observed their leadership style and their approach to leading in the organization, and you want to learn from them. Tell them you are seeking to grow as a leader and that they are the type of leader you most want to be.

Who would turn down a request like that? No Emotionally Agile Leader would turn this down, because they understand that the fundamental role of leaders is not to create followers but to create more leaders.

Now look around you again. Is there someone who seems to be looking for you to be a greater influence on them? Then go speak to them. Don't wait for them necessarily to come to you. Be alert. Be aware. Be emotionally intelligent and emotionally agile, and go seek them out. Offer yourself to them as a mentor.

Make it clear that you want to help them. But make them aware that it will need to be a pull from them and not a push from you. Let them know that you have made the first step, and that was your push, but now they will need to pull—that is, take responsibility for seeking you out and scheduling time for mentoring.

Having been involved in mentoring in both formal and informal formats, I can say that one important task for the growing leader is to come with specific questions and specific scenarios they have already faced or will face in the future. These questions are perfect starters or ice-breakers and will certainly lead to deeper discussions, providing the opportunity for mentors to share real-life experiences.

Dave was a young man who worked for me many years ago when we lived in the Washington, DC, area. He had just mustered out of the Army and was looking forward to beginning a successful civilian career. I knew Dave from church. He was an outstanding young man with a young family and a work ethic I observed and admired long before we ever worked together. As it happened, I was looking to hire an assistant in the small group I was managing. I went to my boss and recommended Dave for an interview and for consideration. Not surprisingly, he was offered the job after the interview. Thus began our business relationship.

I will never forget the first days of working together. Dave would approach my office door, stand to the side of it, knock, and then return to a parade rest. He would also request permission to go to the restroom. Well, we stopped that habit from the Army right away. I made it pretty clear that I was not monitoring or interested in his comings and goings.

We curbed that habit but not his respect and desire to please those who had influence over him. It was clear to me that this young man had as much promise and potential to grow and lead in the civilian world as he had in the military world. And thus began a close business and personal relationship.

Over the next few years, we worked together, talked together, ate lunch together, and spent many hours together at the office. We discussed how the military and civilian worlds were different, what skills would translate from one to the other, and which ones wouldn't. I made sure he had opportunities for exposure to senior management. When given the choice to present something or have Dave do it, I would let him make the presentation.

After several years, I decided to leave the DC area. I had the chance to make a significant career change and move to Houston, Texas. One of the last things I did as I was making that transition was to recommend Dave for my job. Recently, I looked at his profile on LinkedIn and saw how he has grown and leveraged his experiences. He is now in a senior leadership role with a consulting firm whose mission is to assist and advise customers on how to improve their business processes and realize results in the Department of Defense, the intelligence community, and the Department of Homeland Security. Pretty impressive, isn't it? But it all starts with influence—influence that is welcomed by those around you.

But how? How do you do that? By now, you know my love for acronyms and alliterative lists when it comes to writing and organizing my thoughts. So let me offer these words that begin with the letter *I* to guide you.

Intentional. Be intentional in your influence. As I already said, observe those around you and then seek them out. Seeking is an intentional act. You do not stumble upon mentors and mentoring relationships. You must seek them out and act with intentionality.

Involve. Involve the potential leader in as much of your daily activities as is practical. Be careful, though. Sometimes we can overexpose new leaders to too much of the rough and tumble of leadership, which can be disheartening and disillusioning at times. It is sort of like sausage and laws—it's tough sometimes to see how they are made. So involve people, but be careful as well.

Impart. Give them something substantial. Impart to them something real and valuable. Don't just have them sit around and watch you do your leadership thing. Give them something tangible they can use to become a better leader.

Incubate. Incubate? That is an odd word for leadership mentoring. Yes, it is. But it is altogether appropriate if you grasp the context. Provide them with a warm, safe, rich environment for growing them into a leader and developing their skills. Give them a small project or small scope of work where the conditions for success and growth are optimal.

Inspire. Not every aspect of leadership is glorious. Sometimes, we will have to inspire a person to continue on their leadership journey. Remember the quote at the beginning of this chapter? "Teach them to yearn for the vast and endless sea."

Swim Lanes

My family was not a member of the competitive swimming community, so I have only been to a few swim competitions in my life. But I have always been incredibly impressed by the sport and the high degree of personal responsibility even young swimmers have at their appointed spots and at their appointed times to compete. Maybe we could all learn something from watching a competitive swim meet, and maybe I need to take a Sharpie and write a few things on my forearms to help me remember where I need to be and when I need to be there. That is an entirely different topic. But let's consider the swim lanes.

The pool is marked with a series of lines on the bottom of the pool and ropes and floats on the surface of the pool to indicate where each swimmer must remain while competing. Each swimmer wants to get from point A to

point B with the shortest elapsed time, and simple geome-
try tells us that the shortest distance between two points is
a straight line. Therefore, swimmers try to stay within the
swim lane. There is also a penalty for deviating from their
assigned swim lane, which may even mean disqualification
from the race. And even worse, swimmers could cross over
into another swimmer's lane and cause them to break their
rhythm and lose the race.

In a similar manner, it is important to help emerging
leaders recognize their own swim lanes and stay within them.
Outside of the pool analogy, these so-called leadership swim
lanes are usually similar to the person's natural giftedness in
certain areas. Is the person naturally gifted as a communicator?
Then help them stay in that swim lane and maximize their
skill level, becoming better and better as they compete against
better and better "swimmers."

Stretch Assignments

Here is where things get a little difficult. How do I identify
what a stretch assignment would look like for this emerging
leader? Ask them. If you have been intentionally involving,
imparting, incubating, and inspiring them, they probably
already have an idea of what a stretch assignment would look
like for them. So don't be afraid to ask them.

According to Josh Bersin with Deloitte Consulting LLP,
a stretch assignment is a project or task beyond an employee's
current knowledge or skill, given to them in order to stretch
them developmentally.[3] The stretch assignment challenges
employees by placing them in uncomfortable situations so
they can learn and grow. Although this is a general employee
development context, it certainly applies equally, if not more,
to leadership development.

There are five benefits of the experiences gained in stretch assignments for developing and emerging leaders:

- *They are real-world experiences.* If your developing leader has only recently graduated from college or graduate school, they have very limited real-world experiences. All the case studies from their classes pale in comparison to one real, live opportunity to put into practice what they have only studied so far.

- *They are low-cost experiences.* Typically, these experiences are available within the current overall staffing plan of an organization. If your organization rotates new employees through various roles and responsibilities early in their careers, you already have a mechanism in place to provide a stretch assignment. But if you don't, you can still easily provide a stretch assignment due to the normal course of employee attrition or transition without having to add a head count.

- *They are low-risk experiences.* These assignments are low-risk because of the oversight and safety net you will be providing. And you will be providing that, won't you? The overall risk is low because the developing leaders are still operating under your guidance. Therefore, they won't get too far flung if everyone stays open to communication and feedback.

- *They are high-reward experiences.* These assignments offer tremendous and rewarding experiences to the developing leader. They will potentially become some of the experiences that leaders will reflect on at the end of their long careers. And the rewards to the organization are there as well—they provide fresh blood to a leadership pool that may be more stale than fresh.

- *They are disruptive experiences.* This is the natural follow-up to the high-reward experiences. These developing leaders from some of the leading colleges and universities may be closer to the innovative and collaborative environment. That will begin to influence or disrupt the status quo of the organization and challenge some of the ways we have always done things.

CONCLUSION

Becoming an Emotionally Agile Leader

The greatest leader is not necessarily the one who does the greatest things. He is the one that gets the people to do the greatest things.
—Ronald Reagan

You can do this. I believe in you. I know you want to. You just gotta get after it.

There you go. That is my motivational pitch. It may work. It may not. But I have tried in this book to educate, inform, entertain, and inspire you to become an Emotionally Agile Leader. The world is full of various types of leaders who have varying levels of success at creating more leaders and leading organizations to become all they were envisioned to be. Some are more autocratic. Some are more inclusive in their style. Both will work. And oftentimes, a great leader has to take a different approach since each situation is unique. And that is part of the main thrust of this book—a great leader is agile and adaptive in their approach.

Finally, this book was written for the leader who is yearning to be a better leader. One of the first pieces of advice my editor gave me was to create characters and back stories that represent the audience I am trying to reach. That was great advice. So I created Sean, Jim, and Steve. They are just characters in my head, but they each have a story and a reason to become an Emotionally Agile Leader. Let me introduce you to them.

Sean

Sean is 29 years old. He is newly married. He works for a software development company and has just been given the opportunity to lead a software development team on a major project. He didn't ask for the leadership role. It was thrust upon him. Sean will soon find himself leading the same people who are currently his peers. And he is nervous.

He has fairly decent interpersonal skills. But he is a programmer, and programmers are not known to be highly gifted in many of the areas of awareness needed for Emotional Intelligence. He has six weeks before the kick-off meeting for the project and day one of his new leadership role. He knows what his team is going to look like, and they are a crazy cast of characters. What will work in terms of leading one of them will not work with the others. He needs to become an Emotionally Agile Leader.

Jim

Jim is 33 years old. He is married with one child and is a first-line supervisor at a manufacturing company. He has been a supervisor for two years, and he is not getting the best performance out of his team. If he is honest, he would say he is not getting the performance out of himself that he exhibited in the past.

Jim is able to communicate and has a successful marriage. But work is not going how he wants it to, and that is starting to affect him at home. He wonders why things work well at home but are not translating to the office. He needs to become an Emotionally Agile Leader.

Steve

Steve is 31 years old. He is single. In fact, he just broke up with his fiancée after a seven-year relationship. It didn't end well, and if he is honest, he would say that things aren't that great at work, either. The main problem is that he was totally unaware of how he comes across to those he works with as well as those closest to him.

He works for an oilfield services company, and the oil economy is wreaking havoc on his company. It is starting to lay off staff, and he is looking for something to make him more valuable to the company—something that differentiates him from the masses. He knows there will always be a place in his company for those who can lead through this tough time. He is just not sure he is that kind of person. He needs to become an Emotionally Agile Leader.

Sean, Jim, Steve, and You

You and I have much in common with Sean, Jim, and Steve from an emotionally agile perspective. I have told you about them because they represent the many emerging and developing leaders I get to interact with on a daily basis. Their challenges show the need for leadership development in the area of emotional agility.

Nothing New

There is quite possibly nothing new or earth-shattering that you have read so far. In fact, as we have seen, many practitioners of emotional intelligence will tell you that empathy plays a huge part in becoming emotionally intelligent. The ability to adapt to changing market conditions or to the ebbs and flows of the emotional conditions of those around us is driven by our ability to empathize with what others are facing.

Emotional agility is best described as the ability to adapt quickly and decisively. Go back for a few moments to the opening analogy I used about the rockhopper penguin. Following that analogy, an Emotionally Agile Leader can be defined as follows:

> The Emotionally Agile Leader takes the awareness and knowledge of Emotional Intelligence and applies those skills—including the awareness of themselves and of others—to adapt themselves to the ever-changing leadership landscape. Emotionally Agile Leaders recognize that they cannot change how the waves of emotion crash upon the shores of their situations. Emotionally Agile Leaders change the way they face those crashing waves.

You have to get out there onto the rocky cliffs and shores, just like the rockhopper penguin, and try. You cannot be afraid of how you will look in doing so. I am reminded of what Adlai Stevenson once said: "It's hard to lead a cavalry charge if you think you look funny on a horse."[1]

Of course, you should practice self-awareness—one of the four key facets of Emotional Intelligence. But do not let the concern of looking silly keep you from being the leader you want to be and need to be.

I am also reminded of the words of Ralph Waldo Emerson. He reminds me of why I get up every day and do what I do. I close with his words: "Our chief want in life is somebody who shall make us do what we can."[2]

APPENDIX

The Emotionally Agile Leader Methodology

Leadership is modeled, not taught. It must be lived out and demonstrated before our very eyes if it is to impact followers and those who yearn to be leaders. If it is true that leadership must be modeled, and I believe it is, then it is incumbent upon me to provide this section on mentoring with intentionality.

Mentoring is not a mass production process. It is done more in the style of an artisan or craftsman who painstakingly creates works of art one at a time over a substantial period of time.

Mentoring to become an Emotionally Agile Leader is a six-step process with three basic principles undergirding the process. At the very highest level, it can be summarized in the following principles and process.

Principles

We Need to Identify a Leader Worthy of Following

Not every leader is worthy of following. We must understand that from both the leader's and the follower's perspective. As a follower, I must find a leader worthy of following whose successes are not compromised by their ethics or methods.

And as a leader, I must always be diligent to be worthy to be followed.

We Must Learn How They Lead

What is the secret to their success as a leader? What makes them worthy to be followed? And what are they doing specifically that makes them successful as a leader?

We Must Then Lead Others as They Do

After we learn, we must do. Leadership is not an academic pursuit. It is a practical matter, and we must take what we have learned and apply it to our leadership situation.

Process

Story—What Is Your Story?

We all have a story. Each of our protégés has a story as well. There is value in sharing our stories and the journeys that have brought us to the point of a leader-protégé relationship.

Our story is our story. No one can claim it. No one can take it from us. And no one can argue with an authentic story. It may be mundane up to this point, or it may be compelling. Regardless, it is worthy of celebration.

Unique. Our story is uniquely our own. And importantly, it is dynamic. The story of your life up to this point does not have to be the story of the rest of your life. You have the power to change your story and create a whole new plot with all new characters.

Stories are powerful because they show who we are and how we came to be the leaders we are. They reveal the major and minor characters of our lives and show how people have influenced us to be the person we are today. In reality, who we are is shaped by the way our story has been fleshed out in our lives.

Origin. How much of our story is genetic and how much is environmental is up for much debate, and I will not weigh in on that debate here. But this much I know—we are the authors of much of our story. We may not get to create all the characters (you cannot choose your family), but we can write the end of the story. We have the ability to take a set of characters and the plot we have been given and make them into something beautiful and inspiring.

Judgment. Mentoring is not judging. No one wants to be judged. You may not necessarily agree with your protégé's story, but don't judge it. Remember, it is unique to him or her. The cast of characters was different from yours. The plot twisted in ways your plot did not. So affirm your protégé as much as possible.

Bridge. Build a bridge or be a bridge from the past chapters of another person's story to their future chapters. Relationships are the bridges between what is behind and what lies ahead.

Commit. Commit to your protégés that you will always have their best interests at heart. You will create an open and safe place for them to share their thoughts. But they will need to commit as well. As the mentor, you have something they need. You have experience and insights into being an Emotionally Agile Leader—and this experience is what brought you together initially. So commit to a dialogue and to writing a new and better ending than what was being written before.

Connect. Make sure you and the protégé exchange phone numbers and email addresses. After your initial meeting, be sure to connect with them later that day or the next day to follow up with your thoughts and insights.

What Is Your story? What Is Your Protégé's Story? Share Them with Each Other.

Let's go back to the quote attributed to Ralph Nader: "The function of a leader is to produce more leaders, not more followers." The leadership implication is clear. This intentional mentoring is a transfer of leadership skills from one individual to another, all the while preserving and maintaining the skill level of the mentor. In fact, it in no way depletes the reservoir of leadership skills—it deepens them.

Introspection—Leader, Perceive Yourself

Self-awareness is the next step in the Emotionally Agile Leader methodology. It is built on the foundation laid out in books such as *Emotional Intelligence 2.0* and other works that deal with EI/EQ. The mentor helps the protégé come to understand and develop a realistic view of themselves.

Mirror. Be a mirror for your protégé. Help them see themselves for who they really are. Your job is not to be that kind of magnifying mirror we see in hotel bathrooms that magnifies every pore in our skin and points out every flaw. That kind of mirror is designed to help us see better. We just don't always feel better after we see better. What we need to be for our protégé is a mirror that accurately reflects (not magnifies) their traits and characteristics so they can see themselves as others see them.

Perceive. Seeing is not perceiving. We can all see the same event. But we will perceive it very differently based on many factors. You only have to spend a day in a courthouse in any city to see that what our eyes pick up through our optic nerves is not received and processed in the brain the same way from person to person. Witnesses' statements of traumatic events can be wildly different from witness to witness, even though they all observed the same event. Even more confusing is that one person's perceptions and memories of what happened will change over time.

Psychologists often use words like *self-perception*, *perception*, and *meta-perception*, suggesting that we can be good or bad at each type of perception. I am going to modify their words and use some alliteration to help you get a better grip on these terms and their leadership implications. Let's use the terms *self-perception*, *social-perception*, and *circular-perception*.

Self-perception is simply a matter of how you see yourself. Your role as a leadership mentor is to help your protégés see themselves as they really are—not just as they perceive themselves or even as others perceive them. Let's face it. Very few of us have our black belts in self-awareness, so mentors must never come across as having become too much of an expert in this regard.

But what can a mentor do? There are many ways to try to gauge someone's self-perception. I am on record as being a huge fan of 360 surveys and assessments. You can ask mentees to assess their own ability to be self-aware and have a valid self-perception. Then, you can help them take an online assessment and compare the results. How close are the two perspectives?

Accurate self-perception comes from frequent and candid feedback from peers, managers, staff, friends, and followers. Those who seek out this kind of feedback and then take the time to reflect on that feedback tend to have a more accurate or realistic view of themselves. They can also begin to predict how they will react under various stressful or emotional circumstances. They will begin to be able to distinguish people who genuinely like them from people who are using them to further their own agendas. Wouldn't you like to have that kind of clarity?

Social-perception is about taking a step back to look at the social implications and even the motivations of other people. That begins to address the children's saying about the emotional impact versus the physical impact that takes a toll on us. We need to know what the sticks and stones are and what the words are that can hurt us and our leadership efforts.

The danger here is that we become too clinical in our approach and subjugate or deny our own emotional state and response. Instead, work with your protégés to help them pick up nuanced words and tones. They need to be able to spot the nonverbal clues that can help them better understand the social settings of life. They must be perceptive on multiple levels.

Cyclical-perception deals with how we feel about how we perceive others are feeling about us or about an event. In other words, it is your perception of other people's perceptions of you. Do you get it? It can become a cycle of how I initially perceive something, then how I perceive that you may perceive it, and then how I perceive what I perceive about how you are perceiving it. It is almost like looking in those carnival mirrors. But it is really nothing more than the skill of reading the audience, of understanding how others will behave, or of predicting how they will react to an emotional event.

How Perceptive Are You?

Alas, this is not just a leadership development issue. It is not isolated to the young and the still-developing leader. Pride and ego can cloud our perceptions to such an extent that nothing we perceive is valid. But being a master perceiver is a valuable skill in any walk of life, especially for a developing and aspiring leader.

Commit. Commit to your protégé that you will help them on this journey of self-awareness. You will point out their strengths with objectivity and their weaknesses with grace and mercy. Commit that you will help them see instead of just accepting what you see.

Connect. Make sure you provide opportunities throughout the week for protégés to be introspective.

What have you learned about yourself? What is your protégé learning about themselves? Share what you have learned with one another.

Discipline—Leader, Control Yourself

Self-management is the natural next step in this process. The protégé works with the mentor to develop the emotionally agile habits that lead to better self-control.

As difficult as accurate self-perception can be to achieve, self-control may be even more difficult for an emerging leader to achieve. There is a tendency to view whatever we do—emotional outbursts, talking when we should be listening, commanding when we should be questioning—to be perfectly normal and acceptable since we are the leader.

Discovery. Working with our protégés, we must help them discover for themselves what we have come to know. They must realize that self-control is one of the foundational stones upon which leadership is built. In order to lead others, you must first learn to lead yourself.

Management. Emotional self-control is the ability to manage disturbing or conflicting emotions and still remain an effective leader. Self-control allows us to lead effectively even in stressful situations. Notice that I said "manage." Emotions are different from actual conflicts. I always want to resolve conflicts—not manage them.

But self-control (management) is different from suppressing our emotions. We need a full spectrum of emotional responses. It is from that spectrum that we experience the joys of life and the fight-or-flight response. Self-control gives us the time and space to process the extreme ends of the emotional spectrum.

Research shows that leaders who effectively manage their own emotional responses tend to have a much better outcome.[1] If your venture is commercial, then that self-control impacts the bottom line. If your venture is nonprofit or volunteer staffed, then your volunteers show increased commitment or devotion to the cause because of your self-control. If your venture is just your family and friends, ask yourself whether you want to be around someone who is under control or someone who is an emotional ticking time bomb.

Commit. Commit to your protégé that you will help them on this journey of self-control. You will stay close enough to them that when they go through an emotionally charged situation, you will be standing right beside them to help them manage, cope, and control their emotional response. Commit that you will help them be the steady hand on the wheel.

Connect. Make sure you stay close enough to your protégé throughout the week so you can be a resource for them to exercise self-control.

Observe—Leader, Know Your Audience

Never forget that the purpose of mentoring is that the protégé is also a developing leader. Therefore, the mentor helps the protégé quickly assess his or her social situation.

Of the two opportunities to assess—assessing yourself and assessing those you lead—assessing those you lead is the easier of the two. It is not *easy*. It is *easier*.

Listening. One of the most valuable skills for a leader to possess is the skill of being a good listener. But beyond being a good listener is being an active listener. Active listening is full engagement in the conversation. It is listening with your eyes and not just your ears. Your eyes are "listening" to body language. Your ears are picking up not only words but the tone of voice.

I have several generations living in my home, and there is always the sound of voices (noise) coming from various parts of the house and from various people inside the house. It is so tempting to try to block out all the noise. But by listening to those sounds, I discover a wealth of information about how everyone is actually feeling within the walls of that house.

Work with your protégé to develop the skills to assess or read their audience.

Beware of Body Language. The importance of body language is not a hard-and-fast rule for me. Traditional guidance says that if someone's arms are crossed, they are closed to whatever you are saying. I don't believe that to be universally true by any stretch. In fact, I sit that way most of the time. It is the most comfortable pose for me due to my body shape and size. My body positioning in no way indicates what I am really thinking.

Having said that, there are plenty of nonverbal cues available if we will only be a little more alert and perceptive of them. When your audience is constantly checking their watch or Fitbit, are they sending you a message? In fact, imagine for a moment that there is a gigantic, cosmic mute button, and someone has turned off all the sound. Could you determine the tone or context of your audience purely by their body language and mannerisms?

Bubbles. What is the physical distance between you and your followers when you are in their presence? Many refer to this as our bubble. By nature, some folks have almost no bubble. And some have big bubbles that keep lots of physical distance between themselves and those they interact with. Personality preferences aside, once you determine the various ranges of acceptable proximity, you can gauge how close those folks are going to allow you to approach them and how close they will come to you when they are initiating the contact.

Commit. Commit to your protégé that you will go with them to an event or activity to be an extra set of eyes and ears. You can help them assess the audience and then observe the protégé's interactions.

Connect. Make sure you stay close enough to your protégé to be able to observe and assess what they are attempting to observe and assess with their audience.

Influence—Leader, Now Lead Your Audience

The protégé develops skills to maneuver in the social setting to actually lead those around them who are becoming more attracted to their emotionally agile leadership style.

Work with your protégé to resist the urge to begin trying out new leadership techniques and experimenting with various emotional agile leadership principles. None of them will work without first laying the foundation of self-awareness, self-management, and social-awareness. There is no shortcut, and you cannot start with social-management.

It Really Is about Influence. Ask your protégé to consider the following scenario. You have no title of consequence. You have zero power to reward or punish people. Considering that scenario, why would they follow you?

Influence with Impact. They will follow you when you have impacted their life or their interests. Impact means that your leadership has meant something tangible to them. Encourage your protégé to consider what would be most impactful in the areas they are currently leading.

Influence Intentionally. They will follow you when what you do is organized and appears to be done with some forethought. Leadership is not an accidental occurrence. Leaders may arise suddenly in the midst of a great need or tragedy. But long-term leadership is an intentional activity.

Influence with Integrity. It is commonly said that one should use their powers and influence for good, not evil. Similar messages have been given to worthy heroes in movies or TV shows, and the message needs to be said frequently to our protégés. With influence comes great power. It may not come in the form of direct positional authority, but it comes with significant influential authority. So make sure your motives and methods are pure.

Commit. It is important to commit to your protégé that you will help them examine the level of influence they currently possess and the level of influence to which they would aspire.

Connect. Make sure you stay close enough to your protégé to see firsthand what level and style of influence they are exhibiting.

Reproduce—Leader, Make Leaders, Not Followers

The protégé becomes the mentor. This whole process does not demonstrate success until this final step is completed and the process begins anew with the protégé now occupying the role of mentor.

Remember, the goal of a great leader is not to create followers but to create more leaders. This is at the crux of what I am trying to do. I want to create more Emotionally Agile Leaders.

Caught or Taught. That is the age-old method for parents to instill values into their children. These values must be caught, not taught. The same is true for emotional agility. As much as I have written this book to teach, I have really written it so you, the reader, can catch the very thing that has caught me—that there is something to this whole emotional agility and empathetic leadership style.

Commit. Commit to your protégé that you will stay with them in a close relationship as long as necessary in order for them to really catch the Emotionally Agile Leadership model.

Connect. Remain connected through phone calls, emails, text messages, or just sitting down at your friendly neighborhood coffee bar.

NOTES

Introduction

1. Nature on PBS, *Rockhopper Penguins Make Landfall*, September 11, 2014, https://www.youtube.com/watch?v=FwPdmK2EYEk.

2. Travis Bradberry and Jean Greaves, *Emotional Intelligence 2.0* (San Diego: TalentSmart, 2009).

3. Daniel J. Hughes, ed., *Moltke on the Art of War: Selected Writings* (New York: Presidio Press, 1993), 92.

4. Ronald Heifetz, Alexander Grashow, and Marty Linsky, *The Practice of Adaptive Leadership: Tools and Tactics for Changing Your Organization and the World* (Boston: Harvard Business Press, 2009).

5. Bradberry and Greaves, *Emotional Intelligence 2.0*.

Introspective

1. Rafford Pyke, "What Men Like in Men," *Cosmopolitan*, August 1902, https://www.artofmanliness.com/articles/what-men-like-in-men-an-argument-from-1902/.

2. Neel Burton, "What Are Basic Emotions?" *Psychology Today*, January 7, 2016, https://www.psychologytoday.com/us/blog/hide-and-seek/201601/what-are-basic-emotions.

3. "Forrest Gump Quotes," *IMDb*, https://www.imdb.com/title/tt0109830/quotes.

4. Gordon Tredgold, "People Leave Bosses, Not Companies. But Maybe That Boss Is You!" *HuffPost*, January 26, 2016, https://www.huffingtonpost.com/gordon-tredgold/people-leave-bosses-not-c_b_9077466.html.
5. Rudyard Kipling, "If," *Poetry Foundation*, https://www.poetryfoundation.org/poems/46473/if---.

Disciplined
1. Daniel J. Hughes, ed., viii.
2. Warren G. Bennis, *Why Leaders Can't Lead: The Unconscious Conspiracy Continues* (San Francisco: Jossey-Bass, 1997), 158.

Influential
1. Capt. Chesley "Sully" Sullenberger, "What I Got Back," *Parade*, October 11, 2009, https://parade.com/106621/captchesleysullysullenberger/11-what-i-got-back/.

Proliferative
1. Although there is no definitive source for this quote, it is commonly attributed to Antoine de Saint-Exupéry.
2. "Ralph Nader Quotes," *BrainyQuote*, https://www.brainyquote.com/quotes/ralph_nader_110188.
3. Used by permission of Deloitte Consulting LLP.

Conclusion
1. Adlai Stevenson, quoted in Ronald Keith Gaddie, *Born to Run: Origins of the Political Career* (Lanham, MD: Rowman & Littlefield Publishers, 2004), 119.
2. Ralph Waldo Emerson, *The Works of Ralph Waldo Emerson, Vol. 6 (The Conduct of Life)*, 1909, *Online Library of Liberty*, http://oll.libertyfund.org/titles/emerson-the-works-of-ralph-waldo-emerson-vol-6-the-conduct-of-life.

Appendix

1. Harvey Deutschendorf, "Why Emotionally Intelligent People Are
   More Successful," *FastCompany.com*, June 22, 2015, https://www
   .fastcompany.com/3047455/why-emotionally-intelligent-people
   -are-more-successful.

ACKNOWLEDGMENTS

Many people have helped make this book possible. In fact, this book has a beginning that goes back more than 20 years, and it is only today that it has come to fruition. The book began at a boardroom table with a very brash young Air Force Captain named David G. Woods. I sat next to him and was as brash as he, if not more so. We were young, and we were fearless. We were not emotionally agile. But this meeting began an extraordinary relationship with David, who would help me turn an organization around and would fight with me in the trenches of leadership. It was this experience that would lead to my passion to write about emotional agility.

Many others have contributed to my leadership development down through the years. I saw leadership firsthand as a young child as I watched my father in many challenging leadership situations. I married into a family of well-established leaders. They were leaders in their homes, at church, in business, and in many other endeavors. Those men and others like them invited me into close and mutually respectful relationships, and they poured their experiences, talents, and knowledge into me. They gave me room to be brash while becoming more refined. They always believed in me, and they trusted my heart and my motives when my performance did not always measure up.

Perhaps the greatest leadership lessons and proving ground for emotional agility have come from my own home. My beloved bride taught me "communication is a wonderful thing." That was her phrase. And as much as I chafed under the strain of trying to learn to communicate, I saw the value of being able to communicate in times of ease and times of difficulty. She is a gifted communicator. If you don't believe me, ask our children—Libby, Jana, and Jacob; and our grandchildren—Hunter, Hailey, and Jaxton. They will confirm every word I say about her.

I also want to acknowledge the cadre of folks who have been a part of my leadership journey for the past several years. This book would not have happened were it not for guys like Dan, who has worked alongside me at two different corporations. Guys like Wes, who helped me refine my message. Rodney, who shared a passion for leadership and encouraged me to write this stuff down. Dave, who saw talent in me and helped me identify key visuals that represented the thoughts in my head, and who introduced me to the folks who would become my publisher. Ragan, who asked great questions and who was tangible in supporting some of my earlier projects. Glenn, who was able to bring his academic prowess to bear on business and leadership challenges. Bill, who challenged me to specific content creation goals and held my feet to the fire. And Jim, who actually made me believe I had a message worth sharing and talent enough to write it. And then there were the women who made this possible. Jane, who helped me through a writing block and got the project moving again, and Carole, who offered such pointed and tangible thoughts about how this stuff worked in the real world.

There was also an editor who came into the picture about 18 months ago. Laurie scared me at first. She is incredibly talented. She took the time to work with me and pull content from me when all I had was a thought or an idea. By the time we were done, I had an outline and the skeleton of another section.

So many more played a part. Coaching clients gave me raw material with which I could create this book. Professional and personal associates offered insight into the book as it took shape. And my audience, or "followers," contributed significantly as I tested bits and pieces of this content on my LeadershipVoices website.

None of this would have been possible were it not for the love and support of my wife, Cathy. She has truly made this possible. She did not contribute words. Instead, she contributed margin to my life and my schedule that gave me the time and the space to write.

Thank you to each of you.

Do You Want to Be a Mentor or Protégé?

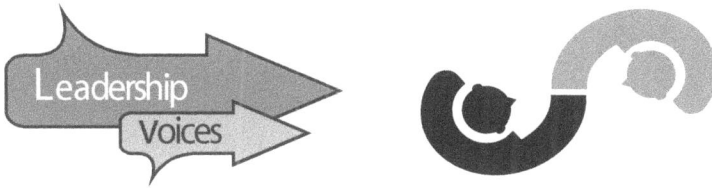

Through the combination of LeadershipVoices and the resources available from The Emotionally Agile Leader, Kevin Bowser will work with you to build your skills as a leader and help you become a better mentor to aspiring, willing leaders. Or, he will work with you as a protégé and help you develop into the Emotionally Agile Leader you want to be.

Kevin is available for:

- Keynotes
- Consulting
- One-on-one coaching

Reach out to Kevin today!

For leadership consulting services and resources, visit http://emotionallyagileleader.com. To join the leadership conversation, visit http://leadershipvoices.com.

Email: Kevin@emotionallyagileleader.com.
Twitter: @TheEALeader
LinkedIn: Linkedin.com/in/kevinbowser/

9 781632 962614